If I Were ~~You~~

A play

Alan Ayckbourn

Samuel French — London
www.samuelfrench-london.co.uk

IF I WERE YOU

First presented at the Stephen Joseph Theatre, Scarborough on 17th October 2006 with the following cast:

Jill Rodale	Liza Goddard
Mal Rodale	John Branwell
Sam Rodale	David Hartley
Chrissie Snaith	Saskia Butler
Dean Snaith	Andrew Brookes

Directed by Alan Ayckbourn
Designed by Roger Glossop
Lighting by Mick Hughes

CHARACTERS

Jill Rodale, early 40s
Mal Rodale, Jill's husband, 40s
Sam Rodale, their son, 15
Chrissie Snaith, their daughter, mid 20s
Dean Snaith, Chrissie's husband, late 20s

SYNOPSIS OF SCENES

The action takes place in the Rodales' comfortable, conventional home. This also serves as an equivalent view of a local showroom of the BFRS Retail Furniture Warehouse.

ACT I
Just before seven a.m.

ACT II
The next morning

Time — the present

Other plays by Alan Ayckbourn published by Samuel French Ltd

ACT I

Three of the rooms in the Rodales' comfortable, conventional home. Just before seven a.m.

First, a view of part of the upstairs (carpeted) master bedroom including a double bed, accessible from either side and a dressing table with stool. One door leading to the en suite bathroom and, ideally, another door to the rest of the house. Second, a view of the downstairs (carpeted) sitting-room including a sofa, coffee table and armchair. All angled to face the (unseen) TV screen. A single doorway to the rest of the house. Third, a view of part of the (lino tiled) eating area of the kitchen, including a table, a section of the fitted units, a sink and a dishwasher, though neither the stove nor the fridge which are out of sight. This room has one door leading to the rest of the house and ideally another, the back door. Overall the house has a tidy, almost unlived in, appearance. Such furniture as we see is well maintained and could indeed be new. There's a feeling that we could be looking at one of those furniture showrooms with their separate room layouts. Which, later on, is what all this occasionally becomes

The bedroom and the sitting-room are in virtual darkness. In the kitchen, the morning sun is just beginning to glow through the blinds. In the bed is Mal Rodale, a man in his forties. Mal is currently fast asleep. Beside him, his wife Jill, a year or so younger, is already awake silently counting the seconds till the alarm goes off. In a moment, it does. Jill cancels it. A beat. Then with a quiet groan she swings her legs out of bed, sitting for a moment in her nightdress, orientating herself. She heaves herself to her feet and walks blearily to the door

Jill (*as she goes; softly; routinely*) Mal … Mal … wake up, now. Time to wake up.

A grumpy muttering sound from Mal, still half asleep under the covers. He does not move

   Jill goes off, sighing

A silence. Then a muttered oath from the bathroom

(*Off; with a cry*) Oh, for God's sake! Mal!

A clatter as the lavatory seat goes down

(*Off*) Is it so much to ask? I mean …

The lavatory flushes

A moment later Jill returns, pulling on her dressing gown

(*Sliding her feet into her slippers; to herself*) Is it so much to ask? Every single morning … (*Addressing the still inert Mal without looking at him*) Mal! Wake up, Mal.

More indecipherable, disgruntled muttering from Mal, under the bedclothes

(*Appearing to understand him*) Yes, well I keep telling you, you shouldn't drink so much, should you?

Jill draws back the curtains. The room brightens considerably as the morning light floods in

Mal (*shocked by this*) Aaah!
Jill (*unmoved*) Time to get up.
Mal (*massaging his head*) Ooooh! Aaaaah!

Jill starts to pad out of the room

Jill (*as she goes; calling*) Sam! Wake up, now! Time to get up!

  Jill exits

After a second, Mal sits up in bed and groans. He seems in some discomfort but this is the way Mal feels every morning first thing and he's used to it. He swings his legs out of bed and groans again, sitting in his T-shirt and shorts

  Meanwhile, Jill enters the sitting-room and, crossing to the windows, draws the curtains here as well. The room brightens

  (*As the light hits her eyes*) Ooooh! (*She studies the view for a second*)

From upstairs in the bedroom Mal begins his early morning throat clearing ritual. Jill hears this through the ceiling. She's used to hearing it but nonetheless she looks up, sighs and moves back to the door

(*As she goes; calling*) Sam! Sam! Time to get up!

Jill goes out

Mal stands and moves to the bathroom, still continuing his loud throat clearing

Mal goes off

Simultaneously, Jill enters the kitchen

(*As she enters; calling back though the door*) Sam! Come on! Wake up! Time to get up!

Jill picks up the electric kettle and empties it into the sink. Upstairs in the bathroom the sound of the lavatory seat slamming up again. More throat clearing from Mal, off. Jill starts to fill the kettle from the tap. Simultaneously, offstage from the bathroom, Mal noisily relieves himself. Jill replaces the filled kettle on its stand. She locates two mugs and gets a couple of tea bags from a container in the cupboard. She places these ready in the mugs by the kettle. She seems to run out of energy at this point and stands totally motionless, staring at the kettle for several seconds waiting for it to boil

After a moment, Sam, their son of fifteen, enters the kitchen. He is half into his school clothes, still barefoot, carrying a bundle of his remaining clothes and his school bag

(*Coming out of her trance; seeing Sam*) Oh, good. There you are.

Sam makes a loud snorting noise in his nose (apparently a subconscious version of his father's own ritual), dumps his stuff on the table and repeats the noise as he goes off again, presumably to the other part of the kitchen

(*As Sam goes*) Don't do that, Sam. You sound like your father.

Upstairs, Mal now has on his white work shirt and boxer shorts. He clears his throat again. He is searching for his socks which he finds on the floor, his side of the bed. He sniffs them cursorily and, finding them satisfactory, sits on the bed and pulls them on, clearing his throat once more as he does so

Sam appears in the kitchen with a soft drink from a newly opened can. He puts the can down and sits, snorting again

Sam!
Sam (*unrepentant*) Sorry. (*He belches as a result of his drink*)

Jill sighs. It is a losing battle. Sam finishes dressing, taking alternate swigs of his drink

In the bedroom, on his bedside table, Mal's mobile rings. Mal, still with one sock on, glances at it and answers it

Mal (*into the phone*) What is it, Sandra? … (*He listens and frowns*) How ill? … Yes, but how ill is ill, Sandra? … (*He clears his throat*) Listen, Sandra, this happens every time there's a —— … oh, yes, it does, my love … yes, it does … it does …

As he talks, Mal goes off, clearing his throat again

In the kitchen, Jill starts laying out a single breakfast place, cereal bowl, etc.

Jill Aren't you going to eat anything?
Sam Mum, can you sign something for me? (*He searches his bag*)
Jill You need more than a fizzy drink …

Sam locates a crumpled school parental permission form in his bag

Sam Here. You need to sign it.
Jill What is it?
Sam Just something to sign. (*He finishes putting on his shoes*)

Jill starts to study the permission form

Mal returns to the bedroom. He has managed, despite continuing his phone call, to get dressed a bit more. He is now searching for something he can't seem to find

Mal (*into the phone; as he enters*) … yes, and you know perfectly well how much I require you there today, Sandra, you know that … I feel let down, my love … well, that's certainly —— … well, that's certainly —— ... well, that's certainly the impression I ... Sandra, every bloody time an audit's due from Head Office ... no, I'm not ... I'm very sympathetic ... *very* ... that's not what I'm saying, Sandra ... no ...

Mal goes out again

Sam is all but dressed now

Jill (*still reading the form*) Shakespeare?
Sam (*casually*) It's nothing.
Jill You're going to be in Shakespeare?
Sam Probably. Maybe. Can you sign it, please?
Jill Don't let your father see this, will you?
Sam No, you can sign it.
Jill (*reading*) A Midsummer Night's Dream.
Sam (*still ultra casual*) It's nothing.
Jill What is it? More of this acting, you mean?
Sam (*rising*) Probably won't even get in it.

Sam pads off in his stockinged feet

Jill (*doubtfully*) Well ... I don't know. You know how your father feels about all this acting, Sam.

The kettle has boiled

Jill pours water on the tea bags and then goes to fetch the milk

Meanwhile, Mal returns to the bedroom, still on the phone. He now has on his suit and one shoe. Locating the other one finally, under the bed, he sits, putting it on with one hand as he talks

Mal (*into the phone as he enters; slightly more irritably*) ... yes, I am ... yes, but only when it's genuine, Sandra ... well, I'm sorry I don't think it is, my love ... I'm sorry ... no, I'm sorry, I don't ... Sandra, listen ... I know all about what women go through, don't bloody give me that, Sandra, I'm married to one, aren't I? ...

Jill returns with a half-full bottle of milk

Jill (*calling through the doorway*) Mal! Tea's here!
Mal (*into the phone*) ... listen ... there's no point in getting hysterical, is there ...?

Jill (*calling again*) Mal! Tea!
Mal (*into the phone*) … listen, I'm not arguing —— (*Yelling irritably through the door*) All right! I'm coming. (*Angrily; into the phone*) … look, just you get your arse into work, Sandra … or you can forget the job altogether, all right? You have been told, girl. Take that as an official warning, Sandra. (*Disconnecting the phone*) Bloody woman.

Mal leaves the bedroom in a bad temper

Jill has finished making the tea. She pours the rest of the milk into a jug and finishes laying out the breakfast place with cereals, sugar, etc.

Sam returns with his shoes

Jill (*as she busies herself*) So what made you want to do this?
Sam (*sitting*) What?
Jill This Shakespeare? What made you want to do Shakespeare?
Sam (*putting on his shoes*) Just for a laugh. She asked me, that's all.
Jill Who did?
Sam Mrs Easterly. She said would I be in it, like, you know.
Jill Mrs Easterly. Which one's Mrs Easterly?
Sam English teacher.
Jill Oh, yes. Tall woman, red hair.
Sam Yeah.
Jill The young one. Quite attractive.
Sam (*shrugging; a bit too casually*) Wouldn't know.
Jill Are you doing it up at the school, then?
Sam No, in the Gardens. It says there.
Jill What Gardens?
Sam Up at the Manor. Hadforth Manor Gardens. It says it all there.
Jill (*impressed*) Oh, those Gardens. I didn't know they had a theatre there.
Sam Open Air. On the grass. Look, just sign it, Mum. I have to bring it back by tomorrow at the latest ——
Jill (*seeing Mal through the door*) Oh, there you are.

Mal enters the kitchen. He is now fully dressed for work in his suit, shirt and tie plus briefcase

Jill immediately picks up the permission form from the table. Sam simultaneously rises as he sees his father and moves away. Mal, still angry, sits at the table without a word and starts to serve himself with cornflakes. Neither of the men acknowledges the other. Sam moves to the door. He has left his drinks can on the table

Don't leave that there, Sam. In the bin. How many more times?

Sam shrugs, takes the can and puts it in the bin. He hovers in the doorway behind his father, signalling to Jill about the form

Time for toast, this morning, have you, Mal?
Mal No.

Mal is suddenly aware of Sam behind him and then of the piece of paper in Jill's hand

What's that, then?
Jill What?
Mal That in your hand?
Jill Nothing.
Mal What is it? Give it here. (*He holds out his hand*)

Jill hesitates. Sam shakes his head at her. Torn, Jill finally hands the form to Mal. Mal reads it. Silence

What's all this then?
Jill It's just …
Mal (*turning to look at Sam*) You want me to sign this?

Sam stares at him

You must be joking.
Sam It's just for fun. For a laugh.
Mal A laugh? There might be time for a laugh when you get your school work right. Judging from your reports of late there doesn't appear that much to laugh about, does there? (*Ripping up the form*) No way.

Sam stares at Mal, then without another word walks out of the door leaving his school bag behind

Silence. Jill gathers up the scraps of paper

Jill (*close to tears*) You don't make things any easier, do you, Mal?
Mal Shakespeare! Poncing about in tights like a fucking fairy …
Jill Mal, don't start! Now, don't start!
Mal (*shouting through the door*) We've got one daughter, we don't want another one, thank you!
Jill Mal, stop it! Calm down!

Sam storms into the sitting-room and throws himself into the chair. We now see just how upset he is. He sits, trying to recover

Both of you. Between you. I can't take much more.
Mal (*slightly calmer*) I've got problems at work …
Jill Yes. Well, stop taking them out on him!

Slight pause. Jill recovers herself

What's the problem at work, then? Another one?
Mal Nothing.

Jill waits

We got the Head Office visit at the end of this week. And bloody Sandra's phoned in sick. Again.
Jill (*supportively*) Oh, she's worse than useless, isn't she?
Mal I told her, if she's not careful she won't have a job. It's common knowledge, they're downsizing. Closing branches here, there and everywhere. Slightest excuse. We could be next. We're on the list. I know for a fact, we're on the list.
Jill You said.
Mal Now him and his Shakespeare! Last in his class, bottom of everything …
Jill Well, that doesn't always follow. So were you at school, weren't you?
Mal That's beside the point. That's no excuse for him.
Jill I was. I was bottom of everything.
Mal That's the reason you have kids. So they can do better than you did. That's the only reason we have them, isn't it?
Jill (*a bit confused by the logic of this*) Well …

Pause

Mal Well, there's always Chrissie.
Jill (*grimly*) We've got two children. Like it or not.
Mal We never had a problem with her, did we? I mean, once we got over the disappointment of her being a girl, never had a problem.

Mal eats for a second. Jill sits silent

Never argued with us. Always did as she was told.

He eats

Worked hard at school, didn't she? Top of her class, she was. Could have done anything. If she'd wanted to.

He eats

Met Dean. Fell in love. Perfect couple. Got pregnant. Happily married.

He eats

What she always wanted. Husband. Baby of her own. Grandchild for you. What you always wanted. Happy ever after. Fairy tale ending.

Jill is silent

Isn't it?
Jill Don't be late now, will you?
Mal We got it right with her, didn't we? So why can't we get it right with him, eh?
Jill He's all right.
Mal He's not all right. He's not right at all. Why isn't he kicking a ball around? Same as other lads? Chasing girls.
Jill You know he doesn't like balls, he never has done …
Mal Well, he should do. He's a boy, for God's sake …
Jill He takes after me. I don't like balls. I've never liked balls.
Mal Prancing around in a park in tights … What sort of thing's that for a lad to be doing?
Jill It might not be in tights, we don't know …
Mal It's Shakespeare, isn't it? They all wear bloody tights. Bunch of shirt lifters.

Mal's mobile rings

Anyway, he's not doing it and that's final! I'm not having a son of —— (*Glancing at his screen*) Oh, I'd better take this. Just a moment.
Jill (*sourly; in an undertone*) Yes, you'd better take it …

He gets up and moves to the door

Mal (*into the phone*) Yes? … Yes … (*Mouthing to Jill*) Just a minute … work.
Jill Yes.

Mal goes out

Jill stands unhappily

(*Sadly*) Oh, dear. (*She looks as if she might cry*) Oh, dear! Oh, dear!

She takes up her own mug of tea and sits at the table. Sam is still slumped in the sitting-room

Mal enters the sitting-room, talking on the phone

Mal (*into the phone*) ... look, I've told you before, love, if you're going to phone me, then don't ever ——

Mal sees Sam and stops talking abruptly

Sam immediately rises and walks straight past Mal and out of the room

Listen, Sam, I ——

But Sam has gone. Mal lowers his voice

(*Into the phone*) It's all right, just someone —— (*Listening*) Yes, I said ... I said, I would ... I *said* ... Why should I say it, then? ... I said it ... I did, I said! ... When? ... When did I ever do that? ... I've never done — *never* ... Come on, don't get like that again ... I've got enough problems, love ...

Mal, pacing, becomes increasingly agitated. He's having a hard time. His increased pacing causes him to leave the room again. He goes out

Simultaneously, Sam enters the kitchen to collect his bag

Jill Sam.

Sam picks up his bag and makes to leave

Sam. Don't just leave without ... Please.
Sam (*turning in the doorway*) I really hate him, you know. I hate him so much.
Jill No, you don't, not really, you're just ——
Sam I'm leaving, Mum. As soon as I can, I'm getting out ...
Jill Now, don't be silly, you can't, Sam, you've got exams coming up ...
Sam I've got to get away from him. You want to come with me, you can.

Jill Sam, he's having trouble at work at the moment, he's ——
Sam Too bad!
Jill He doesn't mean half of it, he ——
Sam And I hate the way he's treating you.
Jill Me?
Sam You know.
Jill What?
Sam You know.

Pause

Mal enters the sitting-room again. He throws his mobile angrily into the sofa. He mouths a silent curse

What you doing protecting him, Mum? Always protecting him.
Jill He's my husband, Sam.
Sam (*sarcastically*) Great!

At this point Dean, late twenties, also in his work suit and tie, bounces in

Dean (*cheerfully*) 'morning, all.
Jill 'morning, Dean. He's in the other room on the phone.
Dean Right. I'll rout him out. 'morning, Sammy boy. (*Aiming a series of shadow punches at Sam's head and body*) Pow! Pow! Boof! Pow! Pow!
Sam (*not reacting; deadpan*) 'llo.

Dean goes off again

Jill Listen, bring another form home tonight. I'll sign it for you. He need never know. They'll let you have another one, won't they?
Sam I don't know.
Jill Come on, Sam. We'll rise above it. We have before, haven't we?
Sam He's not worth it, Mum. Not at all.

Sam leaves

Jill stands

Jill (*despairingly*) Oh, men! Bloody men!

Impulsively, she rushes out

Dean arrives in the sitting-room to find Mal

Dean 'morning!

Mal continues to stare at his phone

You fit then?
Mal Right.

He picks up his phone from the sofa and starts to leave

Dean (*sensing Mal's mood*) OK?
Mal Whatever you do for them, Dean, they're never satisfied, are they? Always wanting more. Whatever you do, it's never enough. You try your best, you work your bloody balls off for them, it's still not enough. You found that out yet, have you?
Dean Well …
Mal (*as he goes*) Give it time, son, give it time …

Mal leaves the sitting-room and Dean follows

Jill enters the bedroom. She has a glass of water. She sits at the dressing table and finds a couple of headache tablets which she pops from their tinfoil into the glass. She watches them dissolve, in one of her trance-like states again

Mal comes into the kitchen, followed by Dean

(*Picking up his briefcase*) Right. Just a tick.

Mal puts the briefcase on the table, opens it and starts rifling through some papers

Dean (*surveying the half eaten cornflakes*) This yours? You haven't finished your cornflakes.
Mal Not this morning.
Dean Oh, I couldn't do that. I always need something to start the day. You know, cooked, like.
Mal What? Egg and bacon?
Dean And the rest. Sausage. Mushrooms. Fried bread. Baked beans. Black pudding. Fried potatoes …
Mal Yes, all right, that's enough …

He concentrates on his task for a moment

What, every morning?

Dean Couldn't start the day.

Mal You're lucky. You must burn it up.

Dean I do. (*Indicating the cornflakes*) Can I finish these?

Mal If you want. (*Giving up his search*) No, I don't seem to have it ...

Dean (*sitting and starting to eat*) What's that?

Mal Invoice from those carpet suppliers. Be somewhere around. I'll find it. (*Puzzled*) Funny, I'm sure I had it ...

In the bedroom, Jill swallows the contents of her glass in one. Under the next, she makes the bed

Mal re-checks his briefcase once more

Chrissie cooks all that for you, does she? Every single day?

Dean Except Sundays. Then I do it. My turn. Boiled eggs.

Mal Fair enough. She doesn't mind, then?

Dean No. Bit tough on her when she was morning sick, but normally ...

Mal How is she, my little girl? How's my Chrystal, then?

Dean Great.

Mal Looking after her, I hope?

Dean You bet.

Mal Little Liam OK?

Dean Magic. He's magic.

Mal That's what I like to hear.

Jill, once she has finished the bed, sits to study herself in the dressing table mirror, pulling at the skin on her face, not liking what she sees

Mal, downstairs, is going through his briefcase contents once again

Dean Big game Saturday, then. (*He finishes his cornflakes*)

Mal Oh, yes.

Dean All hanging in the balance, isn't it?

Mal I'll be there, don't worry.

Dean Wouldn't miss it, eh?

Mal (*giving up his search*) No, Sandra must have filed it. God knows where it is if she's filed it ...

Dean Got a match myself on Sunday. For the Heroes. Last of the season. Hadforth Heroes! Hey! Hey! Hey!

Mal Still in the first fifteen, then?

Dean What? Come on! Could they do without me, could they heck?

Mal I don't know. After that last game …
Dean It was in touch. Fly half was a yard over the line.
Mal Yeah … yeah … yeah …
Dean (*squaring up to Mal; mock aggressively*) Yeah.
Mal (*doing the same*) Yeah? Take you on, any day, kid.
Dean Watch yourself, old feller. Best wait for your mates.
Mal Come on, then.

Mal takes up his briefcase and starts to leave and then stops again in the doorway

> *Under the next, Jill gets up and leaves the bedroom, taking the glass with her*

(*Patting his pockets*) Now — do I have the bloody car keys? — I am getting old, you're right. (*Locating them in a pocket*) Yes, I do. Oh, Dean, by the way … I may need you to — you know — cover for me again, this lunchtime. If you don't mind.
Dean No problem.
Mal I need to sort this out. I'm going to have to sort it out with her today.
Dean No problem.
Mal (*affectionately*) Thanks, mate. You're about the only one I can trust, you know that, Dean.
Dean I'm here for you.
Mal She's a lucky girl, our Chrissie. I hope she knows. (*He pats Dean on the shoulder*) Got herself a diamond, hasn't she?
Dean That's me. Girl's best friend, me. (*As they leave*) You up for a pint after?
Mal I'll need several. Sandra's off sick again, as well …
Dean Sandra? Not again!
Mal Bloody women …

Mal and Dean leave the kitchen

A pause. The house is silent

> *Jill enters the sitting-room. She picks up the TV remote control and points it at the (non-visible) set. A very upbeat announcer's voice is heard*

TV voice (*brightly*) And now coming up shortly, it's time to catch up on the latest goings on at ——

Jill immediately mutes the sound on the TV. The screen continues to flicker. She straightens one or two cushions, inspects the floor critically and leaves the room

In a moment, she enters the kitchen. Moving a little like a sleepwalker, she starts to clear away the empty cornflakes bowl, the cereal packets, milk, sugar, mugs, etc. She stacks the dirties in the dishwasher under one of the units. She wipes the table, gives a final look round and goes out again

The lights change. We are now in the BFRS furniture showroom. The same layout although the items and areas are lit more dramatically with spotlights. The TV stops flickering. There is a background drone of showroom muzak

Mal and Dean enter, in full customer service mode. They both wear earpieces and lapel mics clipped to their suits plus name badges, Dean's with simply his name, Mal's with "Store Manager" under it

Mal (*as they enter, already under pressure*) ... OK, the best short term solution, Dean, is as follows. You stand in for Charlie, here in Beds and Bedding, and I'll keep an eye on Kitchens and Fittings *and* man the office. We'll just have to pray there's not a run on white goods 'cos if there is, we're in deep shit, mate. I'll pull Mary out of Lighting and put her onto Loose Fittings. That'll leave Bald Ron to cope on his own but beggars can't be choosers. Then we've got Big Debbie, God help us, covering Tiles, Rugs and Floor Coverings and she barely knows what day of the week it is anyway, the dozey bitch, but that's the best we can do in the circumstances. All right, got that?

Dean (*a little confused*) I'll stay here, then, shall I?

Mal Don't move. Bloody Charlie. Why did his wife choose today?

Dean I suppose she couldn't help going into labour, could she? I mean ——

Mal Why couldn't she hold the thing in for another three days, till after the audit? I'll give you a call on the radio. Good luck, mate.

Mal steps through what was, until now, the invisible "wall" between the bathroom and the kitchen areas

(*As he goes; into his lapel mic*) Hallo, George. Yes? Well, you've got me, I'm afraid, George ... Sandra's not here this morning ... she called in sick. What's your problem, George, and I hope it's life-threatening, mate, because I don't have time to waste, not this morning ...

Mal goes out through the kitchen door

Dean stands for a moment, in charge of the bedding department. He straightens the cover on the bed proprietorially

Dean (*spotting a customer*) Yes, Madam? Can I be of some assistance?

Dean goes out adopting his dazzling sales smile

The lights change back to normal and the muzak stops. The TV flickers again

Jill enters with the vacuum cleaner. She plugs it into the wall and listlessly starts to vacuum the already spotless carpet. She continues this for some time, giving the impression that she could probably have continued the task for a lot longer, having little else to do

At this moment though, Chrissie, her daughter, mid-twenties, enters and stands in the doorway. Jill, concentrating on her task, is unaware of her for a moment

Chrissie (*above the noise of the vacuum*) Mum? (*Trying again a little louder*) Mum! (*A third try, even louder*) Mum!

Jill finally sees Chrissie

Jill Oh, hallo, love.

Under the next, Jill switches off the vacuum cleaner and starts to pack it away

Chrissie Am I early?
Jill Sorry?
Chrissie I'm not too early, am I?
Jill No, I don't think so. Why?
Chrissie I said I'd be round. Yesterday. We arranged — girls' outing. Remember?
Jill Oh, yes. Sorry.
Chrissie Only you're not dressed. I thought I might be ... a bit early. We said we'd go down the shops, remember.
Jill Oh, yes.
Chrissie You all right, Mum? You look terrible.

Jill Well, I haven't — you know — done my ... I'll make us some coffee. Then I'll get dressed.

Chrissie I'll do that. I left Liam out there. You wouldn't believe it, the minute I get him out of the house, put him in the car, he falls asleep. I think that's what I should do at nights. Drive him round and round the block. (*Taking the vacuum*) Here, I'll take that.

Jill (*releasing the vacuum*) I can manage. You still wouldn't get any sleep though, would you? Not if you're driving ...

Chrissie Joking, Mum, I was only joking.

Jill (*as they go*) Well, I never know when you're serious, Chrissie, and when you're not, these days.

They go out, Chrissie carrying the vacuum

As they do so, the scene changes back to the showroom. The lighting changes and the muzak kicks in again

Mal enters the bedroom whilst simultaneously Dean enters the kitchen. There is an even greater sense of impending emergency

Mal Dean, what the hell are you doing in Kitchens, man? I told you to stay in Bedding!

Dean Sorry, Mal, Enid from Fitted Units, she was looking for you.

Mal You've left Bedding completely unmanned, Dean.

Dean There's a phone call —

Mal — someone could just have strolled in and made off with a king-size.

Dean — for you, she said. Urgent.

Mal I couldn't even get you on the radio. What's happened to your radio, Dean? Don't say it's gone down again?

Dean No, I was in Kitchens, looking for you. You know the radios are rubbish in Kitchens ... it's the aluminium ... Look, Mal, Enid from F.U., she says there's a phone call for you. A Mr Perkins from Eversley — she said he sounded quite agitated ...

Mal (*moving back through the bedroom*) God, who'd be the manager ...?

Dean He said he's hanging on till he gets satisfaction. He'll only talk to you.

Mal What's his name again?

Dean Mr Perkins from Eversley.

Mal Oh, it's that bastard again, is it? I'll soon sort him out, don't worry ...

Dean Now, Mal, don't lose it, mate. It never pays to lose it, Mal ... Not with a customer.

Mal Some of them need thumping. (*As he goes*) And I've had this one up to here.

Mal exits

Dean makes to follow

Dean (*calling*) Someone'll be with you in just one minute, Sir …

Dean hurries off after Mal

The scene changes back again

Jill enters the kitchen with a mug of coffee. She sits

In a moment, Chrissie comes in and joins her

Chrissie No, I say … I was up every ten minutes last night with him.

Pause. Chrissie stares at her mother, aware she is in a state

They say you should leave them to cry, don't they? I've tried that. You just lie there listening to them crying all night. Either way, you never get any sleep.

Pause

Still they say boys are worst, don't they? Sam was the same, wasn't he? I remember he was.

Pause

Yes, boys are worst. Till they get older, then you can scarcely wake them up at all, can you? Dean, he'll sleep through anything, Dean will. Sleeps straight through Liam. All he ever says is "Oh God" and just turns over, you know. Men!

Pause

Mind you, Dad used to get up sometimes, didn't he? For us? Even for me, he did. I mean, I know he used to for Sam early on but … that was different. Sam was always a bit special. But I remember Dad quite clearly. I couldn't have been more than … but I still remember him. If I'd had a bad dream or something. Standing by the bed. Always made me feel so safe. Knowing he was there. It's all right, Chrystal, any monster gets in, he'll have to deal with me first. (*Reflecting*) He's always called me Chrystal. Why'd he start calling me Chrystal, do you know?

Jill (*softly*) He never cared for Christine.
Chrissie Well, no, I don't care for Christine either. But I'm not sure Chrystal's much better, are you? (*She laughs*)

Jill suddenly gets up and hurries from the room

Mum?

Chrissie stands at a bit of a loss. This is evidently an ongoing situation

Now, where did I put my coffee? (*Spying it on an offstage unit*) Oh, yes.

Chrissie picks up Jill's own mug and goes in search of her mother

(*Going out*) Mum?

As she goes, the lights cross-fade to the showroom. Muzak once more

Mal comes into the sitting-room area

Mal (*as he enters; into his lapel mic; irritably*) What is it now, George? Listen, mate, it's your problem, you bloody deal with it, George!

Dean hurries on into the bedroom

Dean How did you get on, then? With Mr Perkins?
Mal Oh, I sorted him out. He won't ring again in a hurry.
Dean You got rid of him, then. How'd you manage that?
Mal I told him to eff off. He says he's going to complain to Head Office.
Dean Head Office? That's in Düsseldorf.
Mal I don't care any more, Dean. His original order's gone missing, as well. Don't know where the hell it is. His word against mine, as things stand. I've been through Sandra's filing but there's no record of a hard copy …
Dean Be on her computer probably.
Mal If you fancy trawling through her spreadsheets you're a better man than I am. I tried ringing her but she's not answering. I've half a mind to go round there and throw a brick through her window …
Dean — er — Mal …
Mal What?
Dean Are you still — you know — going off for — your lunch? Only it's five past.

Mal Oh, God, I'll have to phone her. No way I can leave here now,
is there? (*He stabs a button on his phone*) And, Dean, there's an old
bugger asleep on that Cherry Wood queen-size in the main window.
He's been there half the morning. This isn't a bloody doss house.
Dean Right. I'll kick him off.

Dean goes

Mal connects his phone

Mal (*into the phone*) Hallo, love ... listen, I'm sorry, I'm not going to
be able to make it after all, love, not this lunchtime ... (*A little taken
aback by the reaction*) ... no ... well, so am I, love ... So am —— ...
so am I ... yes, well, no more than I am, love ... I see ... yes, I see ...
oh, no ... no, we can't have that, can we? ... We don't want that, no
... not my little Trixie, no ... (*Under pressure*) ... listen, I'll — I'll
be there in ten minutes, then ... yes, I promise ... ten minutes. Yes ...
'bye-bye, Trix ... yes, I will ... love you, darling ... yes, I love you ...
and I love you ... 'bye. (*Closing the phone*) Oh, shit! (*Calling*) Dean!
Dean, mate! I have to go out, after all ...

*As Mal goes off through the kitchen, the lights change back to the
house and the muzak fades*

*Jill comes into the bedroom and sits in front of her dressing table
mirror. She has been crying and now tries to repair the signs with a
little basic make-up*

*Chrissie appears in the doorway, having followed her up the stairs.
She still holds their two coffee mugs. She puts Jill's mug down on the
dressing table. Jill instinctively moves something under it to protect
the surface. Chrissie sits on the bed and watches Jill for a second*

Chrissie (*at length*) We need to talk about this, don't we?

Silence. Jill does not react

(*Gently*) We do, Mum. I'm sorry, I know you don't like to, but we
do.
Jill Nothing to talk about, really.
Chrissie It's affecting us all.

*Jill shrugs hopelessly. Chrissie, almost subconsciously, rubs her
shoulder*

What about Sam? Don't you care what it's doing to Sam?

Jill (*softly*) Do you think I'd still be here if it wasn't for Sam?

Chrissie There must be something we can do … You're my mother. I hate to see you like this. You look terrible.

Jill Chrissie, saying that doesn't really help, love.

Chrissie Sorry.

Jill He's having an affair, Chrissie. That's all. It's what a lot of men do when they get — to a certain age. They feel — they need — you know — to re-establish themselves.

Chrissie Re-establish themselves? What does that mean?

Jill Ones like your father, anyway. Ones who can't bear to think of it gradually slipping away …

Chrissie Well, Dad's still attractive. Fairly. He's not lost it. Much.

Jill No. And he's out there now, isn't he, proving to himself he hasn't? All the same, he's not the man he was.

Chrissie How do you mean?

Jill He was … (*After a pause; smiling a little*) Then I'm not the woman I was, either. Look at me now.

Chrissie You still look ——

Jill No, I don't. You said. I look terrible.

Chrissie You know I didn't mean ——

Jill And you're quite right, Chrissie. It's six of one, my love. Not all him.

Pause

Chrissie Who is she, do you know?

Jill Oh, some tottie from the make-up counter at Debenhams, I don't know. I don't care, really.

Chrissie Well, you should care. I'd care. If Dean went off and started doing that, I'd … (*She rubs her shoulder again*)

Jill Chrissie, you still love Dean. There's a difference.

Chrissie (*a beat*) And you don't love Dad?

Jill I don't know. Not much. Not really. Not just because of this. That's just a symptom. We've — gone our different ways, you know. As you do.

Chrissie (*unhappily*) I can't bear to think you don't love each other. You're my parents.

Jill shrugs hopelessly. Chrissie sits miserably on the bed

Jill It happens, darling. Nothing special.

Chrissie (*unhappily*) We are though. We're special. I think we are. We were. We used to be.

Jill We'll still be here for you, darling. Even if we separate. You know that. For you and Sam. Your Dad would kill for you. You know he would. If you asked him to.

Chrissie I know. (*Rubbing her arm again*) I don't think that would be a lot of use just at present.

Jill has been observing Chrissie's gesture

Jill What's wrong?

Chrissie What?

Jill You all right? You keep rubbing your shoulder. Is it worrying you?

Chrissie No, not really. Didn't even know I was doing that …

Jill What happened? You strained it?

Chrissie (*dismissively*) No, it's just a bruise. Nothing.

Jill Is it hurting then? You keep rubbing it.

Chrissie No, I just — my shoulder — I banged it on something — nothing.

Jill Let me see.

Chrissie No, it's nothing.

Jill Want some arnica?

Chrissie No, honestly. It's nothing.

Jill I've got some arnica. Sure?

Chrissie It's fine.

Jill You had that bruise the other week, didn't you? On your other arm.

Chrissie I'm a mother. When you're a mother you're always banging into things, aren't you? Comes with the job.

Jill (*unconvinced*) Does it?

She stares at Chrissie for a second

I see. I'll get dressed then.

Jill goes out

Chrissie sits for a second. She rubs her arm again abstractedly

Chrissie (*half to herself*) Better check on Liam …

Chrissie collects up the two coffee mugs and goes off. As she does so, the lights cross-fade to the showroom. Muzak once more

Mal comes from the kitchen

Dean comes from the sitting-room

Mal (*as he enters*) Where have you been now?
Dean I got called away. There was a little bit of a crisis.
Mal Crisis, where?
Dean In Garden Furniture. George — he had a bit of a breakdown. Mrs Armitage sent him home.
Mal Sent him home? She's no authority to do that. There's another hour yet.
Dean Well. To be fair, Mal, I don't think she had a choice. He was sitting under one of the umbrellas, just crying, you know. Didn't look so good for the customers. No option really.
Mal Should have dressed him as a bloody gnome, no one would've noticed the difference. (*He starts to move off*)
Dean By the way — it's a girl, apparently.
Mal What is?
Dean Charlie. His wife had a girl.
Mal (*sourly*) Lucky him. God! Roll on closing time.

Mal marches off through the sitting-room

Dean Seven pounds, three ounces … apparently. Right.

Dean goes off through the bedroom door

The lights change back to the house and the muzak fades

Chrissie comes into the kitchen still with the two coffee mugs. She now starts to rinse and dry these

After a second, Sam enters, still in his school clothes

Sam Oh.
Chrissie Hallo.
Sam You, is it?
Chrissie This'll be me.
Sam Where's Mum?
Chrissie Getting dressed.
Sam Oh. (*Glancing briefly at his watch*) Right.

He dumps down his bag and goes off to the fridge

Chrissie You right, then?

Sam (*off*) OK.
Chrissie How's school?
Sam (*off*) OK.
Chrissie (*continuing with her task*) Good.

Sam returns with a can of soft drink. He sits and watches her

Sam That your baby out there, is it?
Chrissie That's the one.
Sam It's turning blue and choking, did you know?
Chrissie (*unmoved*) Oh, dear. Yes, he does that round about this time of day.
Sam Thought you'd like to know.
Chrissie And his name's Liam. For the hundredth time.
Sam Liam. (*He considers*) That's mail backwards. Did you know that?
Chrissie Yes.
Sam You should write on him, "please forward".
Chrissie (*mirthlessly*) Oh, ha-ha-ha.
Sam If his surname was Layor. L – A – Y – O – R, Liam Layor. Then he'd be Royal Mail backwards.
Chrissie So he would. Only his name's Snaith.
Sam H-tians. Liam H-tians. Not as good, is it? Sounds Dutch. Maybe you should consider changing your name. For the sake of the child.
Chrissie Maybe you should consider changing your jokes. For the sake of my nerves.
Sam (*getting up*) See you, then.
Chrissie See you.

Sam moves to the door, leaving the can on the table

He runs into Jill, now dressed, who enters

Sam Hi, Mum.
Jill Hallo, Sam … Had a good day?
Sam Great.

Sam goes out

Jill sees the can on the table

Jill (*calling him back*) Sam! Back!

Sam reappears

In the bin. Please.
Sam Sorry.
Jill How many times do I have to say it?

Sam returns and puts the can in the bin

I think he's just waking up, Chrissie.
Chrissie Yes, it's nearly time for his feed … I'll give him something.
Sam A food parcel.
Chrissie You'll get a clip round the ear in a minute.
Jill He's been very good. Not a squeak all day.
Chrissie He's saving it for later.

Chrissie goes out

Jill Did you bring another form?
Sam Form?
Jill You know, the permission form? For the Shakespeare?
Sam Oh, yes. Hang on. (*He puts down his bag and rummages through it*) No point though. He'll never let me do it, will he?
Jill He need never know.
Sam He'll find out. Good news is — we had the auditions today with Mrs Easterly and — ta-ra — I got the part I wanted …
Jill Did you? Oh, good.
Sam She said I was right for it and I was. I was brilliant. Here. (*Handing Jill the form*) Hide it from him this time.
Jill I'll sign it now. Got a pen?
Sam Somewhere. (*He produces a pen*) Just sign there and the date.
Jill (*doing so*) Right. If you'd — like me to help you with your words or anything …
Sam (*surprised*) Oh, well, thanks.
Jill Just take you through them, you know. If you want.
Sam May take you up on that, Mum. Maybe tomorrow. See you later … (*He makes to leave*)
Jill Sam …
Sam Yeah?
Jill Do you know yet if you'll be wearing tights?
Sam What?
Jill Only I think it would be easier for your dad if you weren't having to wear tights …
Sam No, I won't be wearing tights.
Jill You won't?
Sam It's not that sort of part.

Sam goes

(*Off*) Goodness me, sister! Are you going to put that huge thing into his little tiny mouth?

Chrissie (*off*) Look, Sam, just sod off, will you!
Jill (*hurrying out*) Now, now, now. Stop that, you two. Sam! Stop teasing your sister …

Jill goes off

As she does so, the lights cross-fade to the showroom

Mal enters through the sitting-room

Mal (*as he enters*) Right, that's it. Closing time. We're off.

Dean comes on through the bedroom

Dean Pub time, then?
Mal Queen's Head, here we come. And I tell you, if Sandra's not here tomorrow … I left her a message on her machine. Be here or die. Come on, then. Are you fit? First one's on me.

Mal goes out through the bedroom

Dean (*following him*) You're on. (*Fumbling for his mobile*) I'd better phone Chrissie, tell her to hold my dinner.

Dean goes out after Mal

The lights cross-fade back to the house

Jill enters the sitting-room, where the TV is still silently flickering away. Jill is drawn to something happening on the screen. She stops to watch

Jill (*as she watches, to herself*) Oh. There now. Oh.

Chrissie enters after a moment

Chrissie What you watching?
Jill Oh, you know …
Chrissie (*recognising the programme*) Oh, yes.

They both stand watching

Jill Ha! I guessed that, didn't you?

Chrissie Yes.
Jill Him and her.
Chrissie Yes.
Jill Bound to happen.
Chrissie Sooner or later. He sleeps with anything that moves. He does.
Jill (*frowning*) Yes.
Chrissie Sorry.

They watch some more

> *In the kitchen, Sam enters with a self-made sandwich in one hand and his copy of "A Midsummer Night's Dream" in the other. He is absorbed in the text in between mouthfuls. He sits at the table*

The two women continue to watch the screen during the next

Chrissie Why do you always watch it with the sound down, Mum?
Jill I think it's more interesting.
Chrissie You can't hear what they're saying, though.
Jill Most of the time you can tell.
Chrissie I suppose.
Jill Leaves you free to get on with other things, then, doesn't it?
Chrissie I suppose so. Dean just phoned. They're in the pub. Surprise! He'll meet me here on his way home.
Jill Hope he doesn't intend to drive.
Chrissie No, it's usually me. (*At the screen*) Oh, God, look, she's going to catch them at it this time, isn't she? She'll chop 'em both up with a meat axe if she catches them, won't she? About time she did. It's been going on long enough. These two. I can't believe she doesn't know by now.
Jill She knows. She's known for ages.
Chrissie You reckon?
Jill You always do. You know it, the minute they start.
Chrissie Oh, look at that. They always cut away to something else, don't they? Just when things are getting interesting.
Jill Well, it's early evening.
Chrissie Yes.
Jill Mind you, later on, they don't cut away soon enough, in my opinion. You want to sit down?
Chrissie Might as well.
Jill (*as they sit*) Get Sam his tea in a minute.
Chrissie Get his own, can't he? His age?
Jill Him? If I don't get him something, I doubt he'd eat at all.

Chrissie You ought to get a job, Mum. You really ought to. Hanging around here all day on your own. No wonder you get depressed. I know I keep saying it, but you ought to get out.

Jill Yes, you're probably right. I think I've lost my nerve, you know. You realize it's been fifteen years since I did a proper job? I mean, I don't count the part-time ones, I mean a *proper* job. You know, proper.

Chrissie Well …

Jill I was good you know. Had a good future. They told me. The youngest Personnel Officer they'd ever appointed. Not even called that now, is it? Human Resources, or something. It was all your fault.

Chrissie Me?

Jill If you hadn't come along …

Chrissie Don't blame me. I'm going back. Soon as he's in nursery school. I'm back to work. I'm not hanging around.

Jill Unless you decide on a second.

Chrissie We'll see.

Jill looks at her for a moment

Jill Listen, if there's anything you want to talk over, Chrissie. You know …

Chrissie Yes, OK.

Jill I'm here.

Chrissie OK.

Silence

(*At the screen*) Oh. Look at that. They're at it again.

Jill I'm amazed she has the energy.

They watch for a second

Chrissie It's nothing I can't cope with, don't worry, Mum.

Jill There's always something you can't cope with, love.

They continue to watch the TV

> *In a moment, Dean enters the kitchen through the back door*

Sam is still reading at the table, mouthing the words silently. Dean is slightly drunk

Dean (*cheerfully*) 'evening. 'evening, Sammy boy! (*Aiming a series of shadow punches at Sam's head*) Pow! Pow! Boof! Pow! Pow!

Sam (*continuing to read, without looking up*) She's in the other room.
Dean What you doing? Homework?
Sam Just reading.
Dean What's this, then? Dirty book, is it?
Sam Pretty dirty. Shakespeare.
Dean Shakespeare! Bloody hellfire! (*As he goes*) Shakespeare! Who does he play for, then?

Dean goes out again

Sam continues to read

Jill (*at the screen*) I always like this one. He makes me laugh.
Chrissie He's even funnier when you can hear what he's saying.
Jill You can tell from his face, though, can't you?

Dean appears in the sitting-room doorway

Dean Right. I'm here.
Chrissie (*without turning*) Hallo.
Jill Hallo, Dean. Mal with you?
Dean Putting the car in the garage. What are you watching, then? (*Staring at the screen*) Oh, this rubbish. You coming?
Chrissie In a minute. It's nearly over, this.
Dean You've got the sound down. Why've you got the sound down?
Chrissie Mum prefers it with the sound down.
Dean You can't hear it with the sound down, can you?

Dean takes up the remote and points it at the TV

Chrissie Dean! What are you doing?
Dean Teletext. Want to see the scores, do you mind?
Chrissie Mum's watching this.
Jill (*muted*) Doesn't matter.
Chrissie (*angrily*) No, come on. Give it here. Dean!

Dean evades her grab for the remote

Dean Oh, look at that! Three – nil.
Chrissie Sorry, Mum.
Dean (*switching the TV back*) There you are! Back to normal. (*He tosses the remote on to the sofa beside Jill*)
Chrissie (*giving up*) Come on, then. I'll drive.

Dean I'll drive.
Chrissie Not with Liam in the car, you're not.
Dean Give us the keys …
Chrissie I'm driving. Look at you, practically falling over …
Dean I am not. Listen, don't make out I'm drunk.
Chrissie (*kissing Jill*) 'night, 'night, Mum.
Dean Don't tell me I'm drunk, girl, when I'm not.
Chrissie (*moving to the door*) Come on then …
Dean No, that really pisses me off, that. When you talk like that.
Chrissie (*embarrassed by his behaviour*) Dean! Come on, please!
Dean No, do you know that? It really pisses me off.
Jill Don't talk to her like that, Dean.
Dean What?
Jill She's your wife. Don't talk to her like that. Show her a bit of respect.
Dean You just keep out of it, mother-in-law. Please? This is just between us, if you don't mind most awfully.

Jill is silent. Despite the jokey nature of the previous exchange, there is an atmosphere in the room

Thank you. So much. (*To Chrissie*) Come on, then, wife of mine. Let's collect his lordship, shall we?

Dean goes out

Chrissie stands awkwardly

Chrissie (*still embarrassed*) It's just talk. He doesn't mean it.

Chrissie fumbles through her bag for her car keys

Jill I hope he doesn't.

Jill rises and moves to Chrissie. She hugs her, nearly catching her daughter off-balance

Chrissie (*wincing*) Ow!
Jill Sorry. Forgot.
Dean (*off*) Come on, then! If you're coming. We want our dinner.
Chrissie See you tomorrow, eh?
Jill See you tomorrow. And we will do the shops. Promise.

Chrissie goes out

Jill moves back into the room. She sits, deep in one of her trance-like states

In a moment, Mal enters the kitchen. He has his briefcase and a takeaway

Sam is still sitting at the table reading, totally absorbed

Mal Hey, Sam. Listen ——

Sam rises at once and makes for the door

Listen, son, I'm sorry about this morning, I was probably ——

But Sam has gone

(*Angrily*) Don't fucking walk away from me when I'm talking to you! (*Slamming the takeaway on the table*) Jesus!

In the sitting-room Jill, hearing this, runs to the door

Jill (*calling*) Sam! Sam!
Sam (*off; as he passes the sitting-room door; yelling*) Forget it!
Jill (*going off after him*) Sam!

Dean appears in the kitchen doorway

Dean All right, Mal?

Mal stands, gripping the table, breathing deeply, trying to calm down

Problem, is there? Mal?

Chrissie appears in the kitchen doorway, long enough to take in the tableau

Chrissie We'll be in the car. Don't be long.

Chrissie goes out again

Mal She has poisoned that boy against me. Do you know that?
Dean Jill?
Mal He was a good boy. Gutsy. You know. Real fighter. Took on anyone. When he was five. Now look at him. Half way to — It's her. It's all her doing that. All of it.

Dean Well …

Mal starts to unpack his takeaway during the next and puts it to re-heat in the offstage oven

Mal It's all her doing, you know. Kept giving him books for Christmas. Storybooks. Dolls.
Dean Dolls?
Mal You know. Toy people. He's a lad. He doesn't want all that. Then it was a doll's house. He had a bloody doll's house when he was five. Had his head stuck in it, jabbering away to himself for hours. Till I took it away, chucked it on the tip. Now it's theatre.
Dean Theatre. Well.
Mal Theatre. When he was born, you know, I had this dream, the way you do, you know, as a bloke does with his son, it's only natural — something a woman, she'd never understand — but you'll know what I'm talking about, Dean, I know you will, what with having Liam and that — I was determined Sam'd grow up and do things I never could. Never had the opportunity to do. Good job, not like mine you know, better than that — professional — maybe shine at some sport or other, you know. I wasn't even bothered which. Football preferably, obviously, but if not … Just so's I could point at him and say, that's my lad, there. Now, what's he doing …?
Dean Shakespeare.
Mal What?
Dean He was reading it just now. Shakespeare.
Mal Enough to break your heart, isn't it?

A car horn sounds outside

Dean I'd better be going.
Mal (*clasping Dean's shoulder*) Thank God for you, Dean. You and Chrissie and little Liam. My hope for the future, mate. You three. Don't let me down. Or I'll come looking for you.
Dean (*squaring up to him*) Oh yeah?
Mal (*doing likewise*) Yeah!
Dean Yeah!
Mal Yeah!

Mal thumps Dean's shoulder. They smile

Dean See you tomorrow.
Mal Tomorrow, mate.

Dean starts to leave

Mal And Dean … (*Pointing at him*) I'm holding you to that.

Dean points a finger back at Mal in a final gesture of male solidarity and finally goes

Jill appears in the bedroom. She has changed back into her night things. She turns down the bed

Mal, meantime, goes off

In a moment, he re-enters the sitting-room. He carries with him his now opened takeaway (a curry), a spoon and fork and an open can of lager. He sits on the sofa. He stares at the silent TV screen and scowls with distaste. He plays with the remote until he finds something he fancies

Jill leaves the bedroom again

Jill (*off; calling*) Sam! Sam!

Mal hears her but ignores it. Instead he eats, drinks and watches TV

Mal (*to the screen*) Go on, girl, go for it! Yes! Whooaarr!

In a moment, Jill enters the kitchen. She glances round and, seeing it empty, she straightens a chair or so and goes, taking Mal's briefcase with her

The lights snap off in the kitchen. Mal continues to eat, drink and watch TV. Jill appears in the sitting-room doorway. She looks at the TV and looks away in distaste. Mal is probably aware of her but doesn't acknowledge her

Jill I'd have cooked you something, you know. I had something in. I could have made you something. You only needed to ask.
Mal (*still watching the TV*) I'm fine.
Jill Well, I expect you had lunch, did you? I expect you had a good lunch?
Mal I had a sandwich.
Jill Oh, dear, mustn't miss out on your lunch, must you?
Mal I won't.

Pause

Jill (*suddenly, angrily; snatching at the remote control*) And would you mind not watching things like that when I'm in the room, please? Would you mind?

Jill darkens the TV screen with the remote which she throws back on the sofa

Mal Hey! What you doing? What's wrong with that?
Jill (*as she goes*) And Sam's locked himself in his room again. I don't know what you said to him this time.

Jill goes out

Mal takes up the TV remote and brings back the TV picture with the sound up loud. A burst of cheesy music. Mal watches for a second but the magic, such as it was, has gone out of his viewing. He switches the TV off again. He goes back to his dinner but after one more mouthful gives up

Mal (*re-tasting the food*) That's bloody revolting, that is.

Jill enters the bedroom. She has removed her dressing gown. She sits on the bed in her nightdress. She starts to cry quietly

Mal swills the rest of the lager, slams down the can and goes off swiftly, abandoning his half eaten meal on the coffee table

The lights snap off in the sitting-room. Jill hears Mal coming up the stairs. She swiftly moves to the dressing table and starts to remove what little make-up she has on

Mal enters the bedroom

During the next there is a long, long silence. Not a look, not a word exchanged between them. Mal comes and goes, as he gets undressed. Jill continues with her face. From the bathroom the sounds of the lavatory seat slamming up and of Mal relieving himself, cleaning his teeth, etc. Finally Jill gets into bed. She turns off her light and lies back, staring at the ceiling

Mal returns in his T-shirt and shorts. He gets into bed beside her and switches off his own light. Pause

Jill (*at length; from the darkness*) We have to talk, Mal.

Silence

Mal, we have to. We do.

Slight pause

Mal There's nothing to talk about, is there?

Mal turns over, his back to her

Jill (*softly*) Oh, God help us.

A silence. Dawn starts to creep up, as before, through the downstairs kitchen blinds. The bedroom and sitting-room grow lighter, too

Sometime in the night, though, Jill and Mal have switched personas. Externally, they still look identical but beneath the skin, as it were, Jill now inhabits Mal's body whilst Mal inhabits Jill's. It takes a moment for them both (and us) to realize this. As well it might. For simplicity's sake, both characters despite their changes of persona, will be referred to by their original names, since they are played by the same actor

The alarm rings. In a moment, Mal (now Jill) cancels it. A beat, then with a quiet groan he swings his legs out of bed, sitting for a brief moment, orientating himself. He heaves himself to his feet and walks blearily to the door.

Mal (*as he goes, softly; routinely*) Mal ... Mal ... wake up, now. Time to wake up.

A grumpy muttering sound from Jill, still half asleep under the covers. She does not move. Mal goes off, sighing. A silence. From offstage, a scream from Mal. A moment later he returns in near panic. He clutches Jill's dressing gown in his hand. He stares at himself in the mirror

(*Touching his face; in horror*) What's happened? What's happened to me? Mal! Mal! Wake up! Wake up!

More indecipherable, disgruntled muttering from Jill, under the bedclothes

(*Shaking Jill awake*) Mal, please. Wake up. Help me! Mal! You have to help me ...

Jill sits up in bed

Jill (*grumpily*) What's going on? What do you think you're doing, woman —— (*Breaking off and staring at Mal; aggressively*) Who are you, then? What the bloody hell are you doing in here, mate?
Mal Mal … it's me. It's Jill.
Jill Jill?
Mal *Jill*. (*Slight pause*) Mal, it is!

He starts to giggle. He stops. The truth slowly dawning on them both

Jill *Jill?* (*Staring at Mal*) Oh, my God.

She lifts the sheet slightly and stares down at herself

(*Looking at him; horrified*) Then who the hell am I, then?

Black-out

ACT II

The same. A few moments later. Mal is still Jill. Jill is still Mal. Mal sits on the stool at the dressing table. Jill sits on the bed. A silence. The first shock is over. Panic is beginning to set in. Particularly for him

Jill I don't know what we're going to do. I don't.

Pause

I can't go to work like this. How can I go out looking like this?
Mal I don't see why not. I went out looking like that.
Jill Ah, but then you were you. Weren't you? Now you're me. And I'm you. Look at me.
Mal Put some make-up on. You'll feel a bit better.
Jill *Make-up?*

Pause

I mean, look at me.
Mal Don't keep saying that. It doesn't help.
Jill I mean — all this ... (*Indicating her breasts*) What am I going to do with these?
Mal I don't know. You were happy enough to stare at them before. You can sit in front of the mirror, now, can't you? Jiggle them up and down to your heart's content. You'll find the novelty soon wears off.
Jill I wish you'd stop making jokes, woman. What the bloody hell is there to laugh at?
Mal Nothing. Absolutely nothing, Mal. I'm sorry, I'm just trying to keep calm. One of us has to. Otherwise I think I'm going to have a panic attack. And that is not going to help either of us, is it?
Jill (*getting up; agitated*) What are we going to do? What the hell are we going to do?
Mal (*also rising*) Mal! Sit down, for God's sake. You're a grown man, now pull yourself together. (*Indicating the stool*) Sit! Sit!

Jill sits

Now listen, I would like you to know that I'm not exactly over the moon at being lumbered with all this, either. All these — extra bits.

I nearly died of fright in there, did you know that? And you left the seat up again.

Jill Sorry.

Mal Well, you won't be doing that any more anyway …

Jill Look, will you just shut up, woman! What are the lads going to say? How can I face them like this?

Mal Well, you can't is the short answer. You'll have to stay here and I'll have to go to work.

Jill You can't do that. You can't do my job.

Mal I'm going to have to try, aren't I? I doubt you can do mine but you're going to have to try your best, as well.

Jill Oh, dear God!

Mal It's the only way, Mal. Think of the kids. Sam. You said it yourself, he's having identity problems. How's he going to react if he discovers his mother's his father and his father's his mother? We have to keep things as normal as possible.

Jill *Normal?*

Mal Look, with any luck it won't last. It may only be temporary. Just a temporary — personality exchange.

Jill Really? I've never heard of that.

Mal No, nor have I but it will have to do for now, won't it? And unless you want to lose your job, I'd better get ready for work. Dean'll be here soon.

Jill Oh, God. How can I face him?

Mal You're not going to have to, are you? I'm going to have to face him.

Jill What am I going to do?

Mal You're going to go downstairs and make sure Sam has something to eat before he goes to school. Then once you've seen him off, you come up here and get dressed. Make yourself presentable.

Jill (*head in hands*) This is a nightmare. I can't do this.

Mal I'll leave you a list of things to do. It's not difficult.

Jill I can't do it.

Mal (*sharply*) Mal! For God's sake, pull yourself together! (*More calmly*) Listen, Chrissie will be round later with Liam. I promised her we'd look round the shops together, you'll enjoy that.

Jill What, you mean dress shops?

Mal What other sort of shops do you look round? By the way, if you want to try anything on you're a size twelve, European thirty-eight.

Jill I'm not doing it, Jill. I cannot do it. I'm sorry. I'll be a laughing stock. No way!

Mal stares at her

*Sam comes into the kitchen half dressed as usual. He dumps his stuff
on the table*

Sam Mum? Mum? (*To himself*) Where is everyone? (*He snorts*)

Sam goes out again, in search of life

Mal All right. If you prefer it then, I'll stay here and you can go to
work. Put your suit on, suck your chest in, try and make your voice
a bit deeper and maybe no one'll notice. Dean or Sandra — or all the
lads you have a drink with afterwards in the pub. Or — the people you
have lunch with.

Jill stares at him

But, then again, even if they do notice — well, you'll have given them
all a *really* good laugh, won't you? So look on the bright side, Mal, I
would.

Jill considers this

Sam sticks his head into the sitting-room

Sam Mum? (*To himself*) Abducted! They've all been abduuucccctted!

Sam snorts again and goes out

Jill (*reluctantly*) Just for today, then.
Mal One day at a time, anyway.
Jill It's not going to work, Jill. Not in a million years.
Mal Why not? Why should anyone ever suspect? Eh? Unless you keep
calling me "Jill", that is.
Jill What am I supposed to call you, then?
Mal Mal, Jill. You call me Mal. And I'll call you Jill, Jill. Or dear. Or
dearest. Or if you're really good, clever girl. Now, go on, off you go
downstairs. (*Handing her the dressing gown*) And I should put this on
or you'll give the postman a heart attack.

Mal goes off

Jill (*appalled*) Bloody hell.

*She pulls on her dressing gown and awkwardly slips her feet into her
slippers, bending to do so*

Oh, heck … (*Straightening; hitching up her bust*) These bloody things weigh a ton, and all.

Jill goes off making the equivalent of Mal's earlier throat clearing noises

Sam comes back into the kitchen. He has the usual soft drink can in his hand. He snorts. He takes out his Shakespeare text again and sits studying it

In the bedroom, Mal comes back dressed in shirt and boxer shorts

Mal (*sniffing his shirt*) Ugggh! Hasn't he a single thing to wear that's clean? He's only got to put them in the basket there, for God's sake. All he has to do!

Mal finds his last night's socks again just by the bed. He picks them up, sniffs them cautiously and recoils

Uggh! I don't believe this. Men! They're animals!

Mal goes off again in search of cleaner socks

Jill meanwhile enters the kitchen. Still clearing her throat

Sam jumps slightly and hides his book

Sam Oh!
Jill 'morning.
Sam Thought you were Dad.
Jill You did?
Sam Yes.
Jill Well, I'm not.
Sam No. I know you're not.
Jill I'm your mum.
Sam I know.
Jill Right.

She takes the kettle and starts to fill it at the sink. The sound of Mal relieving himself in the bathroom upstairs

Mal (*off; horrified*) Aaaaaah, nightmare!

Jill puts the kettle on

Jill Right. Breakfast. What you want? Cornflakes?

Sam No, thanks, Mum. Don't want anything.

Jill Got to have something! Come on! (*Opening the cupboard*) Cornflakes? All Bran? Special K? Muesli? Take your pick. Going, going, gone! Cornflakes, there you are!

Jill bangs the cornflakes packet in front of Sam

Sam (*a little bemused by her brusqueness*) It's OK. I'll just have the drink. I never eat breakfast, you know that, Mum.

Jill produces a bowl and spoon

Jill Bollocks! Most important meal of the day. (*Slamming the bowl and spoon down on the table in front of Sam*) Bowl! Spoon! There you go! Now, eat!

Sam (*startled*) You feeling all right?

Jill What?

Sam You're sounding like Dad.

Jill Am I? Well, I'm not.

Sam (*muttering*) Do without two of you.

Jill (*sharply*) What? What did you say?

Sam Nothing.

Jill Eat!

Sam Right.

Sam serves himself some cornflakes, very puzzled by his mother's behaviour

In the bedroom from his bedside table, Mal's mobile phone rings

Mal enters, now with clean socks on, glances at his screen and answers it

Mal (*into the phone*) Hallo … oh, hallo, Sandra … (*He listens and frowns*) Oh, dear … oh, dear … you're not? … No better? Oh, I'm sorry to hear that Sandra … what's the problem exactly? … Yes … no, I'm feeling fine, no … what's the problem with you? Tell me. (*Listening sympathetically*) … Oh … oh, I see … oh, dear, Sandra … oh, that's horrid for you …

As he talks, Mal goes off

In the kitchen, Jill waits for the kettle to boil

Sam (*still seated*) Any milk is there, Mum?
Jill In the fridge. You know where the milk is.
Sam (*staring at her; rising*) Yes, right.

Sam moves off to the fridge. As he goes he belches as a result of his drink

Sorry.
Jill Better out than in, son.

Jill starts to make two mugs of tea

Sam, during the next, exits then returns with the bottle and sits and pours milk on to his cornflakes

Mal returns to the bedroom. He has managed, despite his phone call, to get his trousers on. He is carrying his shoes. He now sits on the bed during the next and puts them on one-handed

Jill takes the milk from Sam and pours it into the cups on top of the tea bags

Mal (*into the phone; as he enters; still very sympathetic*) ... no, well, as I say ... that can't be normal, Sandra, it really can't be ... not as regularly as that, love ... no ... no ... no, that can't be right ... no, you need to see someone, you really do, Sandra ... no, it's probably nothing at all, love, but you need to be sure, Sandra, don't you ... in your own mind ... (*He listens*)
Sam Any sugar is there, Mum?
Jill Haven't a bloody clue.
Sam Right.
Mal (*into the phone*) ... yes ... mmm ... mmm ...
Jill Better have a look. She'll have some somewhere.
Sam Who will?
Jill I will.
Mal (*into the phone*) ... yes ... mmm ... mmm ...
Sam Right.

Jill and Sam both search the kitchen in both the onstage and offstage cupboards and drawers

Mal (*into the phone*) ... yes, it's a worry otherwise, isn't it ... yes ... you never know the next ... no ... you never know the next ... no ...

you never … no, you never … yes … no, well you can't carry on like this, can you? … No …

Mal goes out again

Jill and Sam are still on their search for sugar

Jill (*producing a box*) Eureka! How about this, then?
Sam That's no good.
Jill Why not?
Sam They're sugar lumps.
Jill It's sugar, isn't it?
Sam You can't put sugar lumps on cornflakes, Mum.
Jill Why not?
Sam Because you can't. It's stupid. You can't put sugar lumps on cornflakes.
Jill (*excitedly*) All right! All right! I'm doing my best!
Sam (*alarmed*) OK. OK. Sorry.

Meanwhile, Mal returns to the bedroom still on the phone. He now has his jacket on

Mal (*into the phone; as he enters*) … yes, all right, Sandra … yes, you phone me the minute you've got an appointment … yes … no, that's all right, my love … the most important thing is to get you right, isn't it …?
Jill Perhaps your — Dad will know.
Sam What?
Jill Where we keep the sugar.
Sam Dad? He won't know. He doesn't know anything.
Jill (*calling through the doorway*) Tea's here!
Mal (*into the phone*) Yes, all right then … I'll wait to hear from you … 'bye, Sandra … not at all … no, you're too valuable to lose, Sandra … 'bye-bye, love.

Mal rings off

Jill (*calling again*) Tea! (*As an afterthought*) Mal!
Mal (*calling through the door*) Coming! (*To herself*) This suit smells like a brewery.

He stands in front of the dressing table mirror for a second. He reaches into a drawer and takes out a perfume atomiser and for a moment is tempted to spray himself with it

He decides to resist the urge and leaves the bedroom

Jill (*frustratedly; giving up her search*) Well, I don't know where it is.
 How the hell should I know where it is?
Sam Don't worry, Mum. I'll eat them without sugar.
Jill Good lad.
Sam You're sure you're OK?
Jill (*snapping*) Of course I'm OK.

Pause

Sam You seem a bit — angry.
Jill Do I?
Sam Tense, you know.
Jill Well, I am tense.
Sam Right.

*Mal looks into the sitting-room, still darkened, shakes his head and goes
and draws back the curtains, sniffing the air distastefully. He sees the
half eaten takeaway and the lager can still on the table*

Mal (*picking them up*) He only has to put them in the bin, all he has to
 do.

Mal leaves the sitting-room

Sam Is it like — you know — like your hormones?
Jill My what?
Sam You know — your hormones?
Jill No, it's not my bloody hormones.
Sam Sorry. (*He eats his cornflakes, rather meekly*)

*Mal enters the kitchen briskly, still carrying the discarded takeaway
and the empty lager can*

Mal (*dumping these in the rubbish bin*) All you have to do — put them
 in the bin. That whole room reeks of stale curry. 'morning, Sam.
Sam (*bemused*) 'morning …
Mal Don't you want some sugar on those? Here.

*Mal produces the sugar container and puts it on the table beside Sam.
He then grabs a can of air freshener from under the sink and a cloth*

  (*Waving the can at them both*) Air freshener. Under the sink for further notice. All right?

Mal goes out

Jill (*after him; rather lamely*) Don't forget your tea, love …

Sam and Jill exchange a look. Jill smiles and shrugs. Sam barely manages to smile back. He is growing rather concerned

Sam What's he doing, clearing up?
Jill Well, he … he must have felt like it.
Sam Have you had a word?
Jill What?
Sam A word? With him? You're always saying you're going to have a word with him. You know — about you clearing up after him.
Jill Yes. I've had a word.
Sam Well done, Mum. Brilliant. (*He eats some cornflakes*)

Jill sips her tea

Mal comes into the sitting-room. He wipes over the table with the cloth, briefly sprays the air with a few squirts of air freshener and leaves again

(*During this*) By the way — did you mean what you said … after school … before he gets back, you know …?
Jill Sorry?
Sam My lines. Going through my lines. In the play. Shakespeare.
Jill Shakespeare. Right.
Sam If you're still on for that?
Jill Yes, I'm — still on.
Sam Hey, I must go. I need to be early this morning. (*Rising*) Thanks for signing the form.
Jill Form? What form?
Sam I should have a lie down, Mum. When we've all gone. You look terrible. See you later.

Mal enters the kitchen

Mal (*as he enters*) Now, Sam, have you had enough …?
Sam (*abruptly*) Bye, Mum …

Sam sweeps past Mal and out of the door

Mal Well, don't just — (*Indicating the table*) Just look at that! Every morning!

Jill (*a little belatedly; after Sam*) Hey, don't just walk away and leave things for your … father.

Mal instinctively starts tidying away Sam's breakfast debris. Jill, equally by instinct, stands watching him

Don't forget your tea.
Mal You're going to have to look out for him, you know. I mean you just can't ignore him any more, Mal. He needs you. Like it or not, you're his mother now and he needs you.
Jill What am I supposed to do? I gave him breakfast.
Mal (*holding up the box*) What? Sugar lumps. Well done.
Jill (*frustratedly*) Oh, I can't cope with this. How can I cope with this?
Mal You're just going to have to. Till we get it sorted out. Look, before I go I'll make you a list. Just the basics. Nothing difficult. I did a big shop at the beginning of the week, we should be all right for food.

Mal takes a kitchen pad and pencil and, sitting at the table, starts to make a list. Jill watches him miserably

Jill (*unhappily*) I don't know how I'm supposed to cope with Sam. He wants me to hear his lines when he gets back. Shakespeare.
Mal (*writing*) You'll have to do it then, won't you? I promised him. You can't let him down. I'll try and keep your end up. You'll have to try and do the same for me.
Jill How are you going to manage at work? Never mind about me. How are you going to manage? It's a complicated job, mine.
Mal Can't be that complicated.
Jill Dealing with people all day. Staff. Managing, motivating them. I had to go on a course. They sent me on a course, you know. Five days.
Mal (*still writing*) I know. I know. You got legless in Prestatyn for a week.
Jill We've got staff off sick. Maternity …
Mal Maternity? Someone had a baby, did they?
Jill Charlie Dilling — in Beds and Bedding. His wife had one yesterday.
Mal Oh, lovely. Boy or girl?
Jill Haven't a clue. Anyway. He's off sick. Well, at least Sandra's back at work. That's one thing.
Mal No, she's not …
Jill After the message I left on her phone last — what did you say?
Mal She phoned your mobile. I've just spoken to her. Told her she was to take time off, see a doctor and get herself sorted out.

Jill You did what?

Mal She's a silly girl. Stuffing herself with painkillers every month …
Where's the sense in that?

Jill Oh, my God! Now what are we going to do … ?

Mal *We* are going to manage without her. (*Holding up the list*) Can you
read that?

Jill What, all this?

Mal Come on, it's perfectly simple. (*Reading*) "One. Make bed." You
can do that, surely. "Two. Vacuum sitting-room and hall … "

Jill What's this one then?

Mal Plumber. Look out for the plumber. He's supposed to come and
look at that cold tap in the kids' bathroom. It's been dripping for
weeks. He keeps promising to come but he never does. Three minute
job. All right? Cope with that?

Jill I don't know …

Mal Well, do your best. Just don't turn your back on him, he likes to
touch your bum. And don't forget Chrissie's round this morning, too.

Jill Shopping.

Mal You'll enjoy that.

Jill Oh, yes.

Mal Seeing Liam.

Jill I suppose.

Mal Of course you will.

Jill Never going to play football with him now, am I?

Mal I don't see why not.

Jill It's not the same. You don't play football with your grandmother,
not if you're a lad. Oh God! There's the match on Saturday.

Mal You can still go.

Jill What, with the lads? Me and the lads? You're bloody joking.

Mal Well, you can go with some of the girls then.

Jill Girls?

Mal Yes. I'll find you a few. One or two I know are quite keen on
football.

Jill (*sitting; sinking her head in her hands*) Oh, no!

Mal Well, suit yourself. Just don't ask me to go with you, that's all.
Once was quite enough … Where's Dean got to? He should be here,
shouldn't he? Listen, go upstairs and put some clothes on. Go on. It'll
be all right, Mal. Don't worry. It'll all be fine.

He kisses Jill on the top of her head

(*Gently*) Off you go. That's it.

Jill gets up and goes slowly to the door

Jill (*hesitating in the doorway*) Jill?

Mal What is it? What's the problem now?

Jill What am I going to wear?

Mal Whatever you like, love, there's plenty in my wardrobe to choose from. Not too casual, not if you're going out later.

Jill A dress?

Mal No. Trousers if you prefer. Try and look a little bit smart, that's all. Don't want to let Chrissie down, do you?

Jill No.

Mal And, Mal, just a little bit of make-up, love. You look terrible.

Jill Right. (*As she goes*) Everyone keeps telling me I look terrible.

Jill goes out

Mal Dear, oh dear. Men!

From his pocket, his mobile rings

(*Retrieving the phone and studying the screen*) Oh. Now, who can this be, I wonder? (*Answering*) Hallo … Oh … yes … hallo, dear … yes … yes … oh, how nice … no, she's not in the room, just me … oh … oh, you must look lovely in that … I wish I could too … I'm glad I bought it for you … yes, it was sweet of me, wasn't it? … Yes … well, we all need spoiling occasionally, don't we? … You more than most …

Dean enters, dressed for work as before

Dean (*cheerfully*) 'morning, all. Sorry I'm late … (*Seeing Mal on the phone*) Oh, beg your pardon, mate … (*He steps back respectfully*)

Jill comes into the bedroom, still clutching her list. She stands for a second. She puts the list down on the dressing table and goes out again

Mal (*still on the phone*) … yes … yes … listen, I'm sorry, dear, I can't talk now. I'm just on my way to work. Yes, I'll talk to you later. 'bye, now. 'bye. (*He rings off*) Sorry about that. Good morning, Dean.

Dean Doesn't give up, does she?

Mal What?

Dean (*indicating the phone*) Don't you give in to her, mate.

Mal I certainly won't.

Dean Treat 'em mean, keep 'em keen, eh? That's my philosophy.

Mal Oh, you find that works for you, do you, Dean?
Dean Sorry?
Mal I'm amazed.
Dean (*laughing; uncertain*) Hey! Watch it? Eh? Yeah? Yeah?

Dean goes through the ritual on his own

Yeah? Yeah! Yeah! (*Running out of steam, rather*) Anyway.

Jill returns to the bedroom. She carries a top and trousers which she now holds up against herself in front of the mirror. They clash horribly. Even she can see this

Jill (*irritably*) Oh, I don't know, do I? How am I supposed to know?

Jill goes out again

Mal finishes tidying the kitchen. Dean sits at the table and watches him

Dean Any road, sorry I'm late. Chrissie and me, last night, we had this slight altercation.
Mal Did you?
Dean Nothing serious. Blow over. You're dead right about women, though, Mal. Seriously.
Mal Am I?
Dean Oh, yes.
Mal Really? I never thought I understood them, at all.
Dean You? You read them like a bloody book, mate, I tell you. (*Sitting*) Like you were saying yesterday, whatever you do for them, they're never bloody satisfied, are they?

Mal finds a dishcloth, wets it under the tap and starts wiping the work surfaces

Whatever you do — whatever you ... (*Noticing Mal*) What you doing?
Mal Just wiping these over.

Mal sets about the work surfaces whilst Dean warms to his theme. Mal shoots Dean the odd venomous look but is evidently trying his best to retain self control

Jill comes back with a second clothes combination which she rapidly rejects as well

She goes out again

Dean (*puzzled*) Oh. No, whatever you do for them … it's never quite enough, is it? I mean, as you said, you try your best, you work your balls off for them, it's still not enough, is it? You were spot on there, mate. I mean take what you're doing now, that bit of cleaning, if she was in here, if Jill was here — don't get me wrong — she'd be saying, oooh, don't forget that bit in the corner, wouldn't she? Or, ooh, look you missed that bit! Wouldn't she? Eh?

Dean laughs. Mal continues, grimly

No, it's all one way, mostly. When you think about it? All about them being appreciated, isn't it? I mean, take last night with me and Chrissie — I mean, don't get me wrong, Mal, I think the world of her — but I mean the entire conversation was about what *she'd* done for *me*. What about all the things I've done for her, eh? I said to her, bloody hell what about all the things I've done for you then, eh? So we finished up having this — this altercation, you know. And this morning, she's still sulking. Refusing to get up. Well, except to feed the baby, of course … So I had to get the breakfast. Do it myself. Boiling eggs … all that.

Mal Nice change for her, anyway. Breakfast in bed.

Dean You're joking. She didn't have breakfast. Wasn't my turn, was it? Fair's fair.

Under the next, Mal finishes wiping the surfaces and, as he passes behind Dean, squeezes the wet cloth over his head

I mean, let's face it, women, they'll turn anything to their own advantage, won't they? To suit themselves? I mean, take the other —— (*Jumping up in alarm*) Hey! What are you doing?

Mal Sorry.

Mal wrings out the rest of the water in the sink and puts the cloth neatly out to dry

Dean Careful.

Mal Ready for off, then?

Dean Sure. Waiting for you. Do you — er — want me to cover for you again, this lunchtime? For your — lunch appointment?

Mal Sorry?

Dean You know. While you — you know — you have your lunch?

Mal Oh, my lunch. No, not today.

Dean No?
Mal Probably — disagree with me.
Dean Right. Sorry. I thought you were … sorry. None of my business.
Mal Come on. We're going to be late.

Dean moves to the door ahead of him and goes out momentarily

(*Checking*) Car keys? Yes. Right. Here I go, then — (*Softly*) Brace
yourself, girl.

Dean returns with Mal's briefcase

Dean Don't forget this.
Mal Oh, thanks.
Dean (*as they go*) How's Jill? Is she any better today, is she?
Mal How do you mean?
Dean Well, she seemed in a bit of a mood, yesterday.
Mal She's in a worse one today, I can tell you …

Mal and Dean leave. From the bedroom, frustrated sounds from Jill

Jill Oh, dammit. Sod you! Do up, you bastard. (*With another effortful
grunt*) Hah! At last.

*A pause. Then Jill comes on, rather red in the face from her struggle,
wearing trousers and putting on a top over her bra*

They're easy enough to get off but they're buggers to put on. (*She
stares at herself for a second*) Well, that's going to have to bloody
do. (*She sits on the stool*) I'm knackered already. (*Catching sight of
herself in the mirror*) God, I do, I look terrible.

*She opens a drawer, then another until she locates some make-up. She
stares at it somewhat bemused*

I don't know. There's tons of the stuff. Decorate a bathroom with all
this.

*A sequence as Jill experiments with a little make-up. The results whilst a
bit haphazard are not as horrendous as they might have been*

(*At length, surveying the results of her handiwork*) There you go.
Gorgeous. Pull anyone now. Now, where's my list? (*Locating it*)
Make bed. Right.

She gets up and pulls the bed over somewhat cursorily. The results would hardly meet with her spouse's approval

That's that then. Piece of piss. Next.

She goes out consulting the list. In a moment, she enters the sitting-room

Vacuum. Where's she keep that?

She picks up the TV remote control and points it at the (non-visible) set. She rattles through about thirty channels at lightning speed, never giving a single programme a chance to settle

No. Nothing. Too early for sport. Not late enough for sex. Vacuum cleaner …

Jill turns off the TV then goes out

A moment later she enters with the vacuum

She plugs it in, as before, and starts going over the floor. After a second, Jill stops and examines the carpet

Not sucking up properly, is it? Not picking up. I don't know. Why can't she keep things maintained? She only has to tell me.

She turns the cleaner over and examines it for a moment

All right, we'll soon sort you out.

Jill gets up and goes to the door

Leave it to a bloke, love. Leave it to a bloke …

As Jill goes out of the sitting-room, leaving the up-ended vacuum cleaner, the lights crossfade to the showroom and background muzak once more

Mal and Dean enter, as before, from the bedroom. They have earpieces and lapel mics clipped to their suits plus their name badges

Dean (*as they enter*) … well, I think the best thing, Mal, if I might suggest, since you're asking me, is to do the same as we did yesterday. I'll stand in for Charlie, here in Beds and Bedding, and you keep an eye on the office as well as Kitchens and Fittings. I mean, if push comes to shove we could always pull Mary out of China again … but that didn't work so well yesterday, did it? I mean ——

Mal What about flowers?

Dean Flowers? We don't have a flower department.

Mal For Charlie's wife? Has anyone organized flowers? I think it would be nice if we sent her flowers, don't you?

Dean (*dubious*) We've never done it before …

Mal Well, I think we should have done, don't you, Dean? Why don't you go round the departments now, make a collection. Have a whip round? I'll phone the florists …

Dean It's not usual. What about Beds and Bedding? Who's going to ——

Mal I'll look after that as well, off you go. (*Touching her earpiece*) I don't know how long I can wear this thing. People keep jabbering in my ear.

Dean You'll need to keep that on, Mal, or you'll be out of contact. You need to remain accessible.

Mal I'll be accessible. Don't worry about that. Off you go.

Dean Right.

Dean starts to go off through the bedroom doorway, shaking his head in amazement

Mal goes out through the kitchen door

Flowers? He's going off his head …

Dean goes off through the bedroom

As he does so, the lights change back and the muzak fades

Jill returns to the sitting-room with a large metal toolbox

Jill (*putting down the toolbox*) This thing's got heavier. Now, then. Let's have a look at you, you little bugger.

She switches off the vacuum at the wall socket and then squats down on the floor and begins to dismantle the machine with a screwdriver

The lights crossfade to the showroom. Muzak again

Mal enters from the bedroom. As he does so, he gets a call via his headset

Mal (*into his headset*) Hallo … who's this, please? Oh, good morning, George … yes … Dean said you might call me … I see … well, I think it's best if you dealt with that yourself, don't you, George? … Well, she's your customer … no, I'm not expecting you to … you can't do better than your best, can you, George? … That's what my mother always told me …

Dean enters through the bedroom behind Mal

Dean (*urgently*) Mal … Mal …
Mal Yes, Dean? (*Into the headset*) … Excuse me one minute, George. … (*To Dean*) What's the problem?
Dean (*grimly*) Mr Perkins. From Eversley. He's back again.
Mal Really? Is that bad?
Dean He's not taking a no. Not this time.
Mal No?
Dean No. He's demanding a yes.
Mal Well, I suppose I'd better talk to him.
Dean I think you'll have to, Mal. He says he's prepared to overlook what you called him yesterday — you know the language — seeing it was in the heat of the moment, like — but he's demanding satisfaction, this time …
Mal Right. (*Starting to move off*) Mr Perkins?
Dean From Eversley.
Mal What did I call him, yesterday, can you remember?
Dean No, but try not to call him anything else, Mal. He's a retired minister and he's not at all happy. Try not to lose it again, won't you?

Mal and Dean go off through the bedroom

As they do so, the lights change back and the muzak fades

In the sitting-room, Jill now has the vacuum cleaner in several pieces

Chrissie enters the kitchen. She wears dark glasses. She puts away her car keys and dumps her bag down on the side and goes out again

Jill (*growling to herself; as she struggles with the vacuum*) Come on … come on, you bastard … yes … you little bastard …

Chrissie, during this, enters the sitting-room, stops and watches Jill with some surprise

Chrissie removes her sunglasses. She has evidently been crying

Chrissie Mum?
Jill Oh, hallo.
Chrissie What are you doing?
Jill Trying to get this thing off. I think there must be a blockage, you
see. It's not sucking up properly. I've managed to strip down most of it
but — Oh, it's a bugger, this last bit. Whoever designed this ...
Chrissie Mum, ought you to be doing that?
Jill It needs fixing.
Chrissie Yes, but do you know what you're doing?
Jill 'course I know what I'm doing ...
Chrissie Don't you think you ought to get a man to look at it?
Jill (*affronted*) What do you mean, a man?
Chrissie Someone who knows. Take it in and have it looked at if it's
not working.
Jill No way. Soon fix this. Don't worry.
Chrissie You sure? You're getting filthy.
Jill Come on, bit of dirt ...
Chrissie It was working yesterday, wasn't it?
Jill Was it?
Chrissie Well, you were using it. Would you like me to help you?
Jill It's no problem. Leave it to me. I'll just get this last bit free and then
we'll get down to the nitty ...
Chrissie Have you checked it's not full?
Jill What?
Chrissie That it doesn't need emptying?
Jill Emptying?
Chrissie It possibly just needs emptying, Mum.

*A long pause. Jill surveys the remains of the vacuum, the various sections
she's removed and finally back to the vacuum again*

Jill (*at last*) That'll probably do it, yes. (*Deflated*) I'll put it back
together, then.
Chrissie No, Mum, don't bother. We'll put it away in the cupboard and
leave it for Dad. Dad can do it.
Jill You'll be lucky.
Chrissie Dad understands these things. I mean, he's useless at most
things but with things like this, he's brilliant, isn't he? Leave it to
Dad, Mum.
Jill (*reluctantly*) Right.
Chrissie Come on, we'll clear it all away and then have a cup of coffee,
shall we?

Jill OK.

They start to collect up the bits

Chrissie Mum, did you mean to wear that today? Do you mind me saying?

Jill How do you mean?

Chrissie That top with those trousers? Was that deliberate?

Jill Yes.

Chrissie Well, it looks a right mess.

Jill Does it?

Chrissie If you don't mind me saying. Terrible. (*She picks up the toolbox*)

Jill No, I'll take that, it's heavy love.

Chrissie (*taking the vacuum with her other hand*) I can manage, Mum. You just bring the bits.

Jill No, Chrystal, you can't carry all that, love, you'll ——

Chrissie (*as she goes*) I can manage … (*As she goes*) Be quiet out here. Liam's just got off.

Chrissie goes off, leaving Jill to bring the loose bits

Jill (*as she follows; muttering*) I wish people would stop telling me I look terrible.

Jill leaves the sitting-room

As she does so, the lights cross-fade to the showroom. Muzak once more

Mal enters from the bedroom doorway. He is answering his phone as he enters

Mal (*into the phone*) … no, I said, I don't think I can come round, not today, I'm sorry … well, we can't always get what we want in this world, can we, Trixie? Particularly when it doesn't even belong to us in the first place … now, don't get like that … Trixie, if you could only hear yourself, love … shouting and screaming like a schoolgirl in a tantrum … quietly, dear, quietly now … you'll make yourself ill … Trixie … Trixie … I'm ringing off now … I'm not talking to you while you're like this … I'll talk later when you've calmed down … goodbye … (*Firmly*) No, I said goodbye, Trixie. (*He rings off*) Dear, oh dear! I thought I was bad enough sometimes.

Dean appears in the kitchen area

All right, Dean?
Dean How d'you get on? With Mr Perkins?
Mal Oh, I sweet-talked him. Don't worry about him.
Dean Sweet-talked?
Mal He was just looking for an argument, that's all. I wasn't prepared
to give him one. I know the sort, I've met them before.
Dean Really?
Mal Oh, yes. Promise them nothing but agree with everything. It's
usually the way to deal with men like that.
Dean Is that a fact?
Mal I'll be in the office if you want me. Looks as if it needs a proper
tidy. Poor Sandra, I'm sure she's a wizard on computers but her
paperwork's a disgrace. (*As he goes through the bedroom*) Customer
over here needing attention, Dean.
Dean (*following Mal off; bemused*) Oh, yes. *Sweet* talk?

Dean follows Mal off through the bedroom

The lights cross-fade back again to the house and the muzak fades

Chrissie enters the kitchen with a mug of coffee

*In a moment, Jill, also carrying a mug, comes in and joins her at the
table*

Jill Sleeping like a log.
Chrissie Told you. Always the same, minute he's in the car. You should
have been round at our place last night. Yelling and screaming.
Jill Real tantrum, was it?
Chrissie I'll say. And that was just us two.
Jill What?
Chrissie Nothing.

Pause. Jill stares at her

Nothing. I've said, nothing you can do. We'll sort it out between us.
We have to.

Jill continues to stare

Nothing. I've said.

Another silence

No, I was thinking about what we were saying yesterday, Mum. I think the problem for Dad, he's like most men, he lives in a sort of fantasy land, doesn't he? Well, they all do really, don't they? In their different ways. Most of them, most of the time. Dean, Sam, Dad. Liam probably eventually. But then we don't help, do we, because quite often we sort of protect them, don't we? Keep the truth from them. Frightened of hurting them, I suppose, little blossoms. I mean. I say things to you, Mum, I'd never dream of saying to Dad. Not in a million years. It's the same with you, isn't it? I mean, this affair of his. You've been playing along with it, but in the end, face it, the only one who's really getting hurt is you. What you should have probably done is said to Dad, "Listen, I know you're having an affair with this woman, so for goodness' sake stop pretending you're not, making all these secret phone calls, pathetically sneaking out in your lunchbreaks as if nobody knew, just go ahead, fuck her senseless and then come back home and let's get on with our marriage, for God's sake." Only you can't really say that to him, can you?

Silence. Jill sits somewhat stunned

You all right, Mum?
Jill I don't know.
Chrissie Sorry. Shouldn't I have said that? I haven't upset you again, have I?
Jill I just feel I've just been run over by a large truck.

Jill suddenly gets up and hurries from the room

Chrissie Mum?

Chrissie stands at a bit of a loss

Oh, God. I can't say a thing right, can I?

Chrissie picks up Jill's mug as well as her own and goes off in search of her mother

(*Despairingly calling; as she goes*) Mum? Mum, I'm sorry …

Chrissie exits

As she does so, the lights cross-fade to the showroom. Muzak once more

Dean comes on from the sitting-room. He sees something off through the bedroom entrance and hurries over

Dean (*calling*) Hey, you, off! Off there! I warned you yesterday!

Mal enters from the bedroom entrance

Mal What's the problem?

Dean Look at him. That old bugger. He's back again in the main window, kipping on the Cherry Wood queen-size ... Hey, you!

Mal No, leave him, Dean. He's an old man, he's not doing any harm. Besides, he's fast asleep. It's a good advert for the bed, isn't it?

Dean Not if he pisses on it in the window, it won't be.

Mal Good point. In that case, go and get him a cup of tea from the machine and wake him up nice and gently, how about that?

Dean Tea? What, in the main window?

Mal Off you go. Good advert.

Dean goes, further bemused

(*Into his headset*) Hallo, George ... back again, are we? ... Now, tell me, how did you get on, George? ... Good, good ... six sun loungers, well done ... you see, you can do it ... A little bit of confidence, all you need ...

Mal goes off through the kitchen

As he does so the lights change and the muzak fades

Jill comes in to the bedroom and sits in front of her dressing table mirror. She is still stunned from her previous conversation with Chrissie

Chrissie appears in the doorway, having followed her up the stairs. She still holds their two coffee mugs. She puts Jill's mug down on the dressing table and sits on the bed

Jill (*at length*) So let's get this straight — she —— ? (*Pause*) He —— ? (*Pause*) I knew all along?

Chrissie That's what you told me.

Jill Yes. Well, I probably did then.

Chrissie You said you did. From day one.

Jill Then why didn't I say something? Do you suppose? To me — to him?

Chrissie I don't know. Sometimes, you know, you both start off talking
about it and it finishes up with him thinking that because you've both
talked about it, he now has your full permission to carry on with it.
You know men. Twist anything to suit themselves, sometimes.

Jill (*a bit mystified*) Oh.

Chrissie You'd lose him altogether, then.

Jill Right.

Chrissie Dad's still a good looking man. Miss Tottie from the make-up
counter, she gets wind you've relinquished your claim, she'll be in
there like a dose of salts.

Jill You reckon?

Chrissie Younger woman, older man. Have him jumping through hoops
in no time, poor bugger.

Jill Probably.

Slight pause

Chrissie Mum … you didn't mean that yesterday, did you? Please
say you didn't really mean it. That you don't love Dad any more?
You didn't mean that, did you? Look, he's a silly, stupid, pig-headed
bloody man and he's treated you so badly he deserves to have it cut
off, but please don't walk away. Give it another go. Think of Sam,
Mum. Both of us.

Jill sits silent

It would break my heart, if that happened, it really would.

Jill rises and crossing, holds Chrissie

Jill It'll be all right, love. I won't let anything happen to hurt you,
Chrystal. I promise.

Still clinging to Jill, Chrissie laughs

What's that?

Chrissie You called me Chrystal. Only Dad calls me Chrystal.

Jill laughs and, growling, gives Chrissie another squeeze

(*Wincing slightly*) Ah!

Jill What is it?

Chrissie Sorry.

Jill All right?

Chrissie Yes, just …
Jill What?
Chrissie (*rubbing her shoulder*) It's just that bruise. Still got it.
Jill What bruise?
Chrissie On my shoulder here. I told you.
Jill (*drawing away from Chrissie*) How did you get it?
Chrissie I said — I banged it on something — Nothing.
Jill Banged it on what?
Chrissie It's nothing. Don't keep going on about it, Mum. I've said. It's nothing. You sort out your own problems. (*Rising*) I'd better go and check on Liam.
Jill (*growing angrier*) Banged into what? Now tell me.
Chrissie I'll be downstairs. (*She turns to leave*)
Jill (*shouting*) Don't fucking walk away from me when I'm talking to you.

Chrissie stops, startled

Sorry.
Chrissie (*after a second*) It's only if he gets a drink or two inside him, that's all. He — he expects things, you know, and I can't — always satisfy him, you know, the way he wants it — just at the moment. I know some women, they get over it just like that. Practically having it away before they're out of the maternity ward but … it's probably partly my fault.
Jill (*shocked*) You control yourself, don't you? If you love your wife and respect her, then you learn to control yourself, surely?
Chrissie I suppose. Nice to think it always happened like that, wouldn't it?

Chrissie goes out

Jill stands frustrated. In a moment, she kicks the bed and leaves the bedroom as well

As she does so, the lights cross-fade to the showroom. Muzak once more

Dean comes on from the kitchen as Mal comes on from the sitting-room. He has some kitchen gloves and some cleaner

Mal I sent off the flowers, Dean. Pass it round the staff, will you? Got a lovely bunch of mixed blooms. Carnations. Roses. Mostly pink, you know. Seeing it's a girl.

Dean (*guardedly*) Lovely, Mal. (*Seeing what Mal is holding*) What you doing, now, then?

Mal Oh, that office is filthy. Filthy. How can anyone bear to work in there …?

Dean Right. You on for a pint later, then?

Mal A what?

Dean A pint? You know, Queen's Head? With the lads?

Mal (*uncertain*) I'm not sure … I'm not sure about that. I'll see.

Mal goes off through the bedroom

Dean (*feebly*) It's my shout … (*As he goes; to himself*) He's lost it. He's completely lost it …

Dean goes off through the sitting-room

The lights change back and the muzak fades

Chrissie comes into the kitchen with the two coffee mugs. She now starts to rinse and dry them

In a second, Sam enters, still in his school clothes

Sam Oh.

Chrissie Hallo.

Sam Here again?

Chrissie Yep.

Sam Where's Mum?

Chrissie Upstairs, I think.

Sam Oh. Getting dressed, is she?

Chrissie No, she's dressed today. Sort of dressed, anyway.

Sam Ah.

He dumps down his bag and goes off to the fridge

Chrissie OK, are you?

Sam (*off*) OK.

Chrissie School OK?

Sam (*off*) OK.

Chrissie (*continuing with her task*) That's good.

Sam returns with a can of soft drink. He sits and watches her

Sam Hey, this'll interest you. Did you know that Liam Snaith …?

Chrissie Oh, God, here we go again …

Sam Liam Snaith is an anagram for Animal Shit, did you know?

Chrissie Do you have nothing better to do at school than sit and make up daft jokes about my child?

Sam I'm interested in his welfare. I'm his uncle, aren't I?

Chrissie God help him. Haven't you any homework to do or something?

Sam I'm going to do this. In a minute.

He produces a book from his school bag

Chrissie What's that?

Sam Shakespeare.

Chrissie Shakespeare. Didn't know you were into that.

Sam I'm in the play. Got a part. Da-da!

Chrissie Does Dad know?

Sam Yeah. Ripped the form up, didn't he? Typical.

Chrissie You're still doing it, though?

Sam Mum signed another one for me. She's going to hear my lines for me.

Chrissie I wouldn't bother her, not today, Sam.

Sam She promised. I'm going to be word perfect before we start. I'm going to amaze them. Mrs Easterly and that.

Chrissie Mum's a bit — a bit out of sorts today, Sam. I wouldn't bother her.

Sam She's always out of sorts. So's Dad. He was this morning. Really, really, *really* odd. Started trying to make me breakfast.

Chrissie Dad did?

Sam Weird. I was so surprised, I almost spoke to him.

Chrissie Something's strange. Can't put my finger on it.

Sam You think maybe they're both — you know — maybe getting senile.

Chrissie Not yet.

Sam It can happen at any age. I was reading. It can happen at your age.

Chrissie No, it can't.

Sam There's senile people of thirty. There was apparently this young woman, she was having a baby and when she woke up from having it, she'd aged seventy-five years ——

Chrissie Oh, bugger off …

Sam (*rising*) True.

Sam moves to the door, leaving the can on the table

He runs into Jill who is about to enter

Hi, Mum.

Sam goes out

Jill Hallo, Sam … I think Liam's just waking up out there, Chrystal.
Chrissie.
Chrissie Yes … I'd better feed him.

Sam reappears

Sam (*smiling sheepishly at Jill*) Sorry, Mum.
Jill What?
Sam (*picking up the can from the table*) Forgot. Sorry.
Jill (*who hadn't noticed*) Oh, well done.

Sam puts the can in the bin

Sam Mum, are you feeling OK to go through my lines, are you?
Jill Lines?
Sam For the play, you know. Like you said.

Jill still looks blank. Chrissie shakes her head at Sam

The Shakespeare. You said you would.
Jill Oh, right. Right. I thought … I thought your Dad said you couldn't
do it?
Sam Yes, he did. Still.
Jill Well …
Sam Never stopped us before, did it? I mean if we only did things he
let us do, things he wanted us to do, we'd never do anything at all,
would we?
Jill No.
Chrissie Sam, don't push Mum. You don't have to do it now, Mum, do
it another day …
Jill No. If I said I'd do it, then I'll do it. If — if I promised.
Sam Great. Thanks.
Chrissie (*softly; to Sam*) Go gently with her.

Chrissie goes out

Sam Shall we go in the other room, then? In case he comes back? Don't
want him interfering, do we?
Jill No.

Sam Just you look …
Jill Terrible. I know.
Sam After you, Mum.

Jill and Sam go off

As they do so, the lights cross-fade to the showroom

Mal enters the sitting-room

Mal (*as he enters; calling*) Oh, Dean …

Dean comes on through the bedroom

Dean That's it then, is it? Home time?
Mal I had a thought, Dean. The staff have worked very hard today. Especially George in Garden Furniture. He really tried his best. I was very proud of him.
Dean George? He's a plonker …
Mal Now, Dean, don't pre-judge people. For all you know, someone's maybe saying that about you somewhere and you wouldn't like that now, would you? Listen … I thought it'd be nice if we bought them all a drink, don't you? Well, on the firm. Buy them all a drink on the firm.
Dean On the firm? You mean everyone?
Mal Be a nice gesture, wouldn't it? I've so enjoyed today, I can't tell you.
Dean There's dozens of them.
Mal Well, push the boat out for once. They won't all come anyway, some of them'll want to get home, I expect, but it's the gesture … (*Into the lapel mic*) Hallo … all departmental heads can I have your attention, please. Would you inform all staff that, as soon as they've finished, Mr Snaith and I will be in the bar of the — (*to Dean*) — where was it — ?
Dean Queen's Head.
Mal — the Queen's Head and we'll be happy to buy you all a drink. Just the one, mind you. (*He laughs; to Dean*) Come on, then. What are you waiting for?

Mal goes out through the bedroom

Dean (*following him*) Right. (*Fumbling for his mobile*) I'd better phone Chrissie, tell her to hold my dinner.

Dean goes out after Mal

The lights change back

Jill enters the sitting-room followed by Sam. Jill sits in the armchair

Jill So. What is it you want me to do?

Sam (*handing her the script*) If you just read the first bit from here —
see, scene two, here — then I'll say my bit and you just stop me if I
get anything wrong.

Jill Right.

Sam I'll stand up. He'll probably be standing up. I mean, we haven't
started yet but I think he'll be standing up.

Sam stands a bit away from Jill, his back to the door

Right. Here we go then. Bit nervous in front of you.

Jill Right. (*Reading*) "Quin: Francis Flute" ——

Sam Quince.

Jill What?

Sam Quin. That's the character's name. It's short for Quince. His name's
Quince. Peter Quince, he's a carpenter ——

Jill That's not a bad trade, you know. Carpenter.

Sam Really?

Jill You could do worse than that. What's he do? The one you're
playing, then?

Sam Francis Flute? He's a bellows maker.

Jill Not a lot of future in that these days, is there? (*Going to read again,
then hesitating*) Listen, son, you're really set on this acting thing, are
you?

Sam Don't know. Maybe.

Jill You enjoy it?

Sam Yes.

Jill Do your — do you have friends who act as well? With you? You
know.

Sam Yes. One or two. Why?

Jill (*casually*) I was just — wondering. Boys are they?

Sam Yes. Some of them.

Jill Girls?

Sam Some girls, yes. You know, to play the girls' parts, like. You
know.

Jill I just wondered if you'd got — you know — other reasons for —
you know — for wanting to be in the play. Like a — you know — a
special friend.

Sam How do you mean? Special friend?

Jill You know like a — like a — girl or something?

Sam No. I don't have many friends that are girls.

Jill You don't?

Sam I find most of them a bit stupid, you know. Talking about their boyfriends. Texting and giggling and that.

Jill But you do have — then — special friends among the boys, do you?

Sam No, no one special. Mum, what's this all about? Why are you asking this?

Jill I was just interested, you know. Interested in you, that's all. I was wondering if you had a special reason for wanting to do something like this, that's all.

Sam I said, I enjoy it. And, you know, because she asked me.

Jill Who asked you?

Sam I told you. Mrs Easterly.

Jill Mrs Easterly?

Sam My English teacher. She asked me and I said OK, I'd give it a go.

Jill Nice, is she?

Sam (*casually*) Yes, she's pretty nice, yes.

Jill Elderly, is she?

Sam About thirty-something. I thought you said you remembered her, Mum?

Jill You tell me about her.

Sam Well, she's tall — pretty tall. Quite thin, you know. (*Describing her with his hands*) Not thin — you know — but in places she's thin … And then she's got quite long red hair and — very green eyes … and — she laughs a lot — great smile … when she smiles at you. You know. (*He stops, rather embarrassed*)

Jill Sounds like you fancy her.

Sam (*smiling*) Wouldn't mind giving her one. (*Immediately penitent*) Sorry, Mum.

Jill rises and moving to Sam, claps him on the shoulder

Jill (*moved*) That's my boy.

Sam (*confused*) I was only joking, Mum, she's a teacher, for God's sake! And she's married.

Jill Well, what's that about, eh? When did that ever — (*Checking herself*) Quite right, lad, quite right. Married woman. Always respect that.

Sam I will. Mr Easterly's the PE teacher. He's huge.

Jill (*sitting down again*) Right. Let's do this Shakespeare.

Sam We'd better. Dad'll be home in a minute.

Jill (*finding her place in the text again*) "Quin —" no, Quince, isn't it?
— "Quince: Francis Flute, the bellows maker."

Sam Here, Peter Quince.

Jill (*reading*) "Quince: You must take Thisbe on you."

Sam What is Thisbe? A wandering knight?

Jill "Quince: It is the lady that Pyramus must love." (*Under her breath*)
Bloody hell, here we go.

Sam What?

Jill Nothing. Carry on.

Sam Nay, faith, let me not play a woman; I have a beard coming. (*Slight
pause*) That's it then, thanks, Mum.

Jill That it? That all you say?

Sam In that scene, yes, that's all he says. Except later on there's an All.
When we all say, "That would hang us, every mother's son."

Jill Not much of a part, is it? This Flute? Doesn't get to say much, does
he? Hey, what about this one later on? This Tita? He goes on a bit.

Sam No, that's Titania, Mum. Queen of the Fairies.

Jill (*hastily*) Oh, well, you don't want to get into that.

Sam No, he says a lot more, Francis Flute, later on when he's doing
Thisbe ——

Jill The woman's part?

Sam Look, I'll show you. Thisbe has this death speech. I nearly know
that. Thisbe's just found her lover, Pyramus, dead, like in *Romeo and
Juliet*, you know, and she's so upset she goes and kills herself then.
Listen. I think I know it. I think I do.

*He positions again and starts to perform for Jill. What Sam lacks
in technique and sophistication, he makes up for in sincerity and
simplicity*

Jill, despite herself, slowly gets drawn in

So. Thisbe comes in. And she sees him, you know, lying there and
then she says:
>   Asleep, my love?
>   What, dead, my dove?
>   O Pyramus, arise!
>   Speak, speak! Quite dumb?
>   Dead, dead! A tomb
>   Must cover thy sweet eyes.

At this stage, Chrissie enters quietly and lingers in the doorway, listening to Sam

> These lily lips,
> This cherry nose,
> These yellow cowslip cheeks,
> Are gone, are gone:
> Lovers, make moan!
> His eyes were green as leeks

… Er … hang on …

Sam hesitates, losing his words, momentarily

Simultaneously, Dean looks in at the kitchen doorway. He is, as yesterday, slightly drunk

Dean 'Evenin' all. We're back. (*Seeing no one*) Oh.

Dean goes out of the kitchen again

Jill Go on, Sam …
Sam Oh, yes. I remember.
> O, Sisters Three,
> Come, come to me,
> With hands as pale as milk;
> Lay them in gore,
> Since you have shore
> With shears his thread of silk.
> Tongue, not a word;
> Come, trusty sword:
> Come, blade, my breast imbrue:

He mimes stabbing himself and falls to his knees

> And farewell, friends;
> Thus Thisbe ends;
> Adieu, adieu, adieu.

Sam lies down on the floor feigning death. Jill and Chrissie watch enthralled

Dean chooses this moment to enter noisily

Dean (*as he enters; loudly*) Excuse me! Just want to catch the half time score, ladies, do you mind …

Chrissie Dean, don't! Sam's doing his ——
Dean Oh, hallo, Sam. What you doing down there, mate? Having a kip?
Chrissie (*holding Dean back by an arm*) Dean, don't —— !
Dean (*shrugging free from her grasp; brusquely*) Don't do that, come on!

Dean moves to the coffee table, stepping over Sam, and picks up the TV remote control

Jill (*rising; furiously*) Don't you interrupt my son in the middle of his Shakespeare, you pillock!
Chrissie (*startled*) Mum!
Sam (*incredulous*) Mum!
Dean Eh?

Jill grabs the remote and tries to wrestle it from Dean

Jill (*angrily*) Give me that, give it to me!
Dean (*winning the tussle*) Come on, let's see the screen. Just for a minute, that's all!

Dean pushes Jill reasonably gently to one side. This is, in retrospect, the wrong thing to do

Jill Don't you push me, you bastard!

Jill throws a punch which catches Dean, totally unprepared, on the jaw. Dean goes down with a crash. Almost immediately, Jill hops about nursing her hand which probably received more damage than Dean's jaw

Chrissie } (*alarmed*) Dean!
Sam   }   Mum!

Sam goes to see to his mother. Chrissie goes to kneel beside the pole-axed Dean

Chrissie Dean! Are you all right? Dean?
Sam Mum!
Jill (*nursing her hand*) Bloody hell!
Chrissie Is it broken?
Jill Feels like it.

Sam I don't think so. You can still move your fingers. That was fucking
   amazing, Mum!
Jill Don't swear in front of your mother …
Chrissie Put something cold on it, Sam, prevent the swelling.
Sam Come on, then, Mum … (*To Chrissie*) Is he still alive?
Chrissie Yes, he'll be all right.
Sam Pity.

Sam and Jill go out

Chrissie tends to Dean

Dean (*sitting up; groggily*) What happened there?
Chrissie She punched you.
Dean Who did?
Chrissie My mother.
Dean Your *mother?*
Chrissie Yes.
Dean My God!
Chrissie Come on, Dean, up you get. We'll go home. I'll fix you
   something to eat.

Chrissie helps Dean to his feet and assists him to the door

Dean (*as they go; incredulously*) Your mother punched me? Your
   mother?

Chrissie and Dean leave the sitting-room

As they do so, Sam helps Jill into the kitchen

Sam Sit down there, Mum. I'll get you something. Frozen peas are best.
   Have we got any peas?
Jill (*sitting*) I haven't the faintest idea.
Sam Wait there.

Sam goes off momentarily

Jill He's got a head like a rock, that lad. Always suspected he had.

Sam returns with a packet of frozen peas

Sam Here!

*He dumps the packet on to Jill's hand, resting on the table. Jill reacts
with a cry*

Sorry.

Jill That's worse than the bloody bruising.

Sam Sorry. (*Looking at Jill through new eyes*) I think you're amazing,
Mum.

Mal enters the kitchen and takes in the scene

Sam continues to minister to Jill's hand

Mal (*only slightly drunk*) 'evening. Had a good day then, dearest?

Jill Wonderful.

Mal Just been out for a quick drink. Sorry I'm late.

*Chrissie comes into the kitchen supporting Dean. Dean stops short in
the doorway as he sees Jill. Chrissie collects her handbag*

Chrissie 'evening, Dad.

Mal (*mystified*) Hallo, Chrissie. Hallo, Dean.

Dean, still in shock, stares at Mal

Dean all right, is he?

Chrissie propels Dean out ahead of her

Chrissie (*as she goes*) Once he's had his dinner. See you tomorrow,
Mum. 'night all.

Sam 'night.

Jill 'night.

Mal (*still mystified*) 'night.

Chrissie returns briefly

Chrissie (*to Sam and Jill*) Oh, don't spread it around what happened
to him, will you? He'd never live it down at the rugby club. Just a
secret between us, all right? If it comes to it, I'll be the one to spread
it around, don't worry.

Chrissie goes out

Mal What on earth's been going on?

Jill Nothing to worry about. I think that's enough of that now, Sam, thanks all the same. I'm beginning to get frostbite. I'll go upstairs in a minute. Run it under the tap. (*Aware that Sam is in the room with them; to Mal*) So you had a good day then, you say? Dear.

Mal Yes, dearest, I think it was — a good day, yes — (*Taking the peas from a slightly startled Sam*) — I'll put those away, shall I, Sam —

Mal goes to the fridge

(*Off*) — We, all of us, we've just been out for a quick drink ...

Jill All of us? Who's all of us?

Mal (*Off*) Anyone who wanted to come. About twenty or thirty of us, in the end ——

Jill Twenty or thirty? Who paid for that?

Mal enters

Mal (*returning*) The firm did.

Jill My God!

Mal Just the first round. Oh, by the way, sorry, I'm afraid I scraped the car getting into the garage just now.

Jill Oh, for ——

Mal Sorry, love. I keep telling you we don't need a car that size, we really don't. And I certainly shouldn't have been driving it after two glasses of white wine, I tell you that.

Jill (*appalled*) You've been drinking white wine?

Mal Yes. It isn't bad at all in there, The Queen's Head.

Jill White wine? In front of the entire staff?

Mal Not bad at all.

Jill (*shaking her head*) I'll be upstairs.

Sam who has been staring at them both, bemused, now makes to follow Jill

No, Sam, you stay here. Have a chat with your — father.

Jill goes out

Mal (*after a slight pause*) Have you had your supper, Sam?

Sam (*awkwardly*) — Er ... no.

Mal I'll cook you something, shall I?

Sam (*alarmed*) — Er, no, thanks, Dad. No way.

Mal I think I've got a couple of instant ones in the freezer. Would you like one of those? There's a chicken or there's a fish one, I think.

You know, the salmon in that sauce. You liked it last time you had it, remember? Well, I heard you — liked it the last time you had it. Your mother said you liked it the last time you had it, anyway.

Sam No, thanks.

Mal Omelette? I'll make you an omelette. Cheesy omelette. One of my fluffies — one of your mother's special — fluffy ones.

Sam What's going on here? You've taken up cooking, Mum's punching the daylights out of people …

Mal At least have a sandwich. I'll make you a sandwich. (*Concerned*) Sam, you must eat something. Please. Please.

Sam stares at him, knowing something is wrong but unable to tell what

Sam (*reluctantly*) OK.

Under the next, Mal locates the ingredients and swiftly and adroitly makes Sam up a sandwich. Sam watches fascinated by his father's newly acquired culinary dexterity

Mal (*as he does this*) What happened with Dean then?

Sam Mum punched him.

Mal (*unsurprised*) Yes, I thought she might. To do with Chrissie, I take it?

Sam No, I was — Dean interrupted my Shakespeare and she decked him.

Mal Good for her. Cheese OK for you?

Sam Yeah.

Mal Shouldn't really. Give you nightmares. You know, tomorrow, as soon as I get home, I'm going to cook us all a proper meal. All of us, sitting down together for once. You, me and — and your mother. (*Completing the sandwich*) There. That'll have to do you for now. Just pop the plate in the dishwasher when you've finished, will you, Sam?

Mal presents Sam with the sandwich

What do you say, then?

Sam Thanks, Mum. Dad. Sorry. Ta.

Sam heads for the door

Mal Sam — you'll do your Shakespeare for me sometime, won't you?

Sam Sure. If you want.

Mal I'd love it. I'll probably go up early tonight. It's been a long day.

Mal instinctively moves to kiss Sam on the cheek but checks himself, in time

'night — son. (*Unconvincingly*) Yeah! Yeah! Yeah!

Mal claps Sam rather awkwardly on the shoulder in a gesture of male solidarity

Sam 'night, Dad …

Sam goes out, still rather dazed

Mal busies himself in the kitchen, tidying up

Jill enters the bedroom, wearing Mal's T-shirt and shorts

Jill (*catching sight of herself in the mirror*) No. Wrong.

Jill goes out of the bedroom again

Sam comes into the sitting-room and sits eating his sandwich and reading his script

In the kitchen, Mal finishes tidying up and now calls up on his mobile. He takes a deep breath

Mal (*getting the answering service*) Hallo, Trixie … it's me … I've just got home … Trixie, I don't know where you are at the moment, why you're not picking up … but I had to call to warn you … Trixie, she knows … she knows all about us … and, Trixie, she's dangerous, love … please God, she never finds out your address. I'd hate for anything to happen to you … she's like a woman possessed … punching people — threatening to kill them, I … Trixie, I can't talk now she's coming back in the — oh my God! What's she got in her hand? Trixie —— (*She rings off, abruptly; muttering*) Sleep well, dear.

In the bedroom, Jill comes back in dressed in her nightdress. She gives herself one more look in the mirror and gets into bed and lies there absently massaging her hand

In the kitchen, Mal gives a final look round and goes out

In the sitting-room, Sam finishes his sandwich, gets up and also leaves the room

Mal (*off*) Goodnight, Sam.
Sam (*off*) Goodnight, Dad.

In a moment, Sam comes into the kitchen with his plate. He puts it into the dishwasher

Mal meanwhile looks into the sitting-room for a look round

Mal Everything off? Good.

Mal goes out again

The lights in the sitting-room go off

Sam (*looking round the kitchen; to himself*) It is. It's aliens. It has to be.

Sam leaves the kitchen

The lights in the kitchen go off

In a moment, Mal enters the bedroom, taking off his jacket. He sees Jill in bed

Mal You've still got your make-up on.
Jill (*dourly*) I know. I'm expecting the plumber.
Mal It's all right for you. You don't have to get the sheets washed, do you?
Jill I think I do now.
Mal Well, suit yourself then.

Mal goes out

Jill (*calling; to Mal*) I plugged my razor in to re-charge. You'll need it in the morning.
Mal (*off*) Thank you. What have you done to my vacuum. It's all in bits.
Jill I was — emptying it.
Mal (*off*) Oh, there's an easier way, you know. You coped all right, then?
Jill All right. (*Reflecting*) Good to talk to Sam again, anyway. Even if he was talking to you.
Mal (*off*) I hear he did his Shakespeare for you?
Jill Yes.
Mal (*off*) Was it good?

Jill Yes — he — was quite good, you know. For a lad, you know. (*Pause*) I can't do this for long, Jill. Staying home all the time. I'll need to get out. Get a job.

Mal (*off*) I'm not stopping you.

Jill Amazing you didn't go crazy all these months.

Mal (*off*) Yes, wasn't it?

The main lights in the bedroom now go off so that it is lit solely by the two bedside lights

Mal enters, dressed for bed in his T shirt and shorts

(*Sitting at the dressing table*) Look, I didn't like to say it earlier but — I wouldn't wear that top with those trousers again, will you, love? I loathe that top, I never wear it.

Jill Then why have you still got it?

Mal (*taking a jar of face cream from a drawer*) Oh, I've dozens of things I hate and I still keep. Never get round to throwing them away. (*Seeing he has face cream on his hand*) No, I don't need this do I? Well, no harm, is there? What the hell.

Mal rubs cream into his face

(*As he does*) Listen, Mal, I have to tell you — whatever happens, I'm going to carry on working, love. Today, I got a taste for it. I mean I was rusty but it all started coming back to me. I felt — ten years younger. I mean, I think I was technically five years older but ... you understand?

Jill Fair enough.

Mal (*getting into bed*) Maybe we could work together.

Jill How do you mean?

Mal I could do with someone in that office. It's chaos in there.

Jill Ah, well, Sandra's off, isn't she?

Mal Hooray! The Queen of Filing ...

Jill Well, I'm not working for you ...

Mal I wouldn't employ you ... Want the light out?

Jill Yes.

Mal I won't sleep, mind you. I never do.

Jill Nor will I.

Mal Oh, ho-ho. That'll be the night.

Together they switch their bedside lights off. The room is in near darkness

(*As they do this*) No, I think honestly, Mal, once I'd got over the initial shock … Chrissie was quite right. I should have gone back to work, ages ago. Re-trained. But, you know, you lose confidence, don't you? After all these years. And if things aren't … I was amazed the way I slipped back into it … some differences, yes. Computers and card machines … but people haven't changed, though … they're still the same, aren't they? … Mal?

Gentle snoring from Jill

Mal? Straight off. How does he do it? (*With a sigh*) All right. Here we go. One sheep … two sheep … three sheep … why do they always have to be sheep? Why not cows for a change? … Or Trixies? One Trixie … two Trixies … three Trixies … four Trixies … five Trixies … six Trixies …

In the darkness, her voice slowly fades out as it first merges with and is then replaced by Jill's voice

Jill … six Trixies … seven Trixies … eight Trixies … nine Trixies … ten Trix —— (*She stops*) Mal? Mal?

Mal is now the one snoring gently beside her. Jill switches on her light again

Mal! Wake up! Mal!
Mal (*sleepily*) What is it? What is it now, woman? I only just got off to … off to … off to … Hang about.

Silence

Jill We've changed back.

Mal switches on his light. He looks at Jill

Mal We have, haven't we?
Jill We have.

They take this in for a second

Mal Thank God for that.
Jill Thank God.
Mal Back to normal.

Jill (*rather sadly*) Yes. Back to normal. What do you think could've —— ?

Mal Don't know. Could have been a dream. Could just have been a dream.

Jill What? Both of us? At the same time?

Mal No, well, maybe not.

Jill Anyway, my hand still hurts like hell, thank you very much.

Mal Sorry, love.

Jill No, you did right. He deserved it.

Mal Well. That's that then, isn't it?

Mal switches off his light again. Slight pause

Jill Mal, we can't pretend it didn't happen. I mean, that would be such a waste, wouldn't it. Everything's changed now for both of us. We can't simply ignore it, can we? Can we, Mal?

Mal No, we need to talk it through, you're quite right, love. We definitely need to talk things through, don't we?

Pause

Don't you think? Jill?

Slight pause

Jill (*snuggling up to him*) In the morning, love. Let's talk in the morning, shall we?

Mal (*holding her to him*) Yes, we'll talk in the morning, love.

As they both lie there contentedly in each other's arms, Jill reaches out and switches off her own light

Black-out

FURNITURE AND PROPERTY LIST

ACT I

On stage: Upstairs carpeted master bedroom, containing:
Double bed. *Under it*: shoe (**Mal**)
Dressing table with mirror. *In it*: headache tablets, make-up, perfume atomiser, face cream
Stool
Door leading to an en suite bathroom
Window with curtains
Slippers (**Jill**)
Socks, mobile (**Mal**)
Downstairs carpeted sitting-room, containing:
Sofa. *On it*: cushions
Coffee table
Armchair
TV remote control
Doorway leading to rest of house
Window with curtains
Lino-tiled eating area of the kitchen, containing:
Sink. *At it*: cloth, tea towel
Dishwasher
Electric kettle
Fitted units. *In them*: mugs, container of tea bags, cereal bowls, cutlery, cornflakes, box of sugar lumps, sugar, jug, air freshener, notepad, pencil, sandwich ingredients
Table
Chairs
Bin
Door leading to rest of house
Back door
Window with blinds

Off stage: Bundle of clothes, two cans of soft drink, school bag. *In it*: permission form, sandwich, copy of *A Midsummer Night's Dream* (**Sam**)
Half full bottle of milk, glass of water, vacuum cleaner, mug (**Jill**)
Briefcase. *In it*: papers. Earpiece, lapel mic, name badge, takeaway, spoon, fork, can of lager (**Mal**)
Earpiece, lapel mic, name badge (**Dean**)
Mug. Bag. *In it*: car keys (**Chrissie**)

Personal: Car keys (**Mal**)
                Mobile phone (**Dean**)
                Second permission form, pen (**Sam**)

ACT II

Set: On **Mal**'s bedside table: mobile phone

On stage: Dressing gown (**Mal**)

Off stage: Two more cans of soft drink, frozen peas (**Sam**)
                Top, trousers, second clothes combination, mug, large metal toolbox. *In it*: screwdriver (**Jill**)
                Briefcase (**Dean**)
                Sunglasses, car keys, handbag, two coffee mugs (**Chrissie**)

LIGHTING PLOT

ACT I

To open: Morning sun glows through kitchen blinds

Cue 1   **Jill** draws back the bedroom curtains   (Page 2)
         Bedroom brightens considerably as morning light floods in

Cue 2   **Jill** draws back the sitting-room curtains   (Page 2)
         Sitting-room brightens

Cue 3   **Jill** points remote control at TV   (Page 14)
         Off stage TV screen flickers

Cue 4   **Jill** exits   (Page 15)
         Cross-fade to dramatic showroom lighting, TV screen
           stops flickering

Cue 5   **Dean** exits   (Page 16)
         Cross-fade to household lighting, TV screen flickers

Cue 6   **Jill** and **Chrissie** exit   (Page 17)
         Cross-fade to dramatic showroom lighting, TV screen
           stops flickering

Cue 7   **Dean** hurries off after **Mal**   (Page 18)
         Cross-fade to household lighting, TV screen flickers

Cue 8   **Chrissie**: "Mum?"   (Page 19)
         Cross-fade to dramatic showroom lighting, TV screen
           stops flickering

Cue 9   **Mal**: "I have to go out, after all …"   (Page 20)
         Cross-fade to household lighting, TV screen flickers

Cue 10   **Chrissie** exits   (Page 22)
         Cross-fade to dramatic showroom lighting, TV screen
           stops flickering

Cue 11   **Dean** exits   (Page 23)
         Cross-fade to household lighting, TV screen flickers

Cue 12	**Jill** exits	(Page 26)
	Cross-fade to dramatic showroom lighting	
Cue 13	**Dean** goes out after **Mal**	(Page 26)
	Cross-fade to household lighting, TV screen flickers	
Cue 14	**Jill** exits	(Page 33)
	Kitchen lights snap off	
Cue 15	**Jill** points remote control at the TV	(Page 34)
	TV screen stops flickering	
Cue 16	**Mal** points remote control at the TV	(Page 34)
	TV screen flickers	
Cue 17	**Mal** points remote control at the TV again	(Page 34)
	TV screen stops flickering	
Cue 18	**Mal** exits	(Page 34)
	Sitting-room lights snap off	
Cue 19	**Jill** turns off bedside lamp	(Page 34)
	Bedside light snaps off	
Cue 20	**Mal** turns off bedside lamp	(Page 34)
	Bedside light snaps off	
Cue 21	Silence	(Page 35)
	Dawn creeps through kitchen blinds, bedroom and sitting-room grow lighter	
Cue 22	**Jill**: "Then who the hell am I, then?	(Page 36)
	Black-out	

ACT II

To open:	Dawn effect	
Cue 23	**Mal** draws back the curtains	(Page 44)
	Sitting-room brightens	
Cue 24	**Jill** points remote control at TV	(Page 52)
	TV screen flickers	
Cue 25	**Jill**: "Vacuum Cleaner …"	(Page 52)
	TV screen stops flickering	

Cue 26	**Jill** exits *Cross-fade to dramatic showroom lighting*	(Page 52)
Cue 27	**Dean** exits *Cross-fade to household lighting*	(Page 53)
Cue 28	**Jill** dismantles the vacuum *Cross-fade to dramatic showroom lighting*	(Page 53)
Cue 29	**Mal** and **Dean** exit *Cross-fade to household lighting*	(Page 54)
Cue 30	**Jill** exits *Cross-fade to dramatic showroom lighting*	(Page 56)
Cue 31	**Mal** and **Dean** exit *Cross-fade to household lighting*	(Page 57)
Cue 32	**Chrissie** exits *Cross-fade to dramatic showroom lighting*	(Page 58)
Cue 33	**Mal** exits *Cross-fade to household lighting*	(Page 59)
Cue 34	**Jill** kicks the bed and exits *Cross-fade to dramatic showroom lighting*	(Page 61)
Cue 35	**Dean** exits *Cross-fade to household lighting*	(Page 62)
Cue 36	**Jill** and **Sam** exit *Cross-fade to dramatic showroom lighting*	(Page 65)
Cue 37	**Dean** exits after **Mal** *Cross-fade to household lighting*	(Page 66)
Cue 38	**Mal** exits the sitting-room *Sitting-room lights off*	(Page 76)
Cue 39	**Sam** exits the kitchen *Kitchen lights off*	(Page 76)
Cue 40	**Mal**: "Yes, wasn't it?" *Main bedroom lights off*	(Page 77)
Cue 41	**Mal** and **Jill** switch off bedside lamps *Both bedside lights off*	(Page 77)

Cue 42   **Jill** switches her bedside light on   (Page 78)
           Bedside light on

Cue 43   **Mal** switches his bedside light on   (Page 78)
           Bedside light on

Cue 44   **Mal** switches his bedside light off   (Page 79)
           Bedside light off

Cue 45   **Jill** switches her bedside light off   (Page 79)
           Black-out

EFFECTS PLOT

Property fittings required: electric kettle, two bedside lamps, vacuum socket

ACT I

Cue 1	**Mal** is asleep. **Jill** lies silently for a few moments *Alarm sounds*	(Page 1)
Cue 2	**Jill** cancels the alarm *Alarm stops*	(Page 1)
Cue 3	**Jill**: "Oh, for God's sake! Mal!" *Clatter as the lavatory seat goes down*	(Page 2)
Cue 4	**Jill**: "Is it so much to ask? I mean ..." *Lavatory flushes*	(Page 2)
Cue 5	**Jill** empties the kettle into the sink *Lavatory seat slams up*	(Page 3)
Cue 6	**Jill** starts to fill the kettle **Mal** *noisily relieves himself*	(Page 3)
Cue 7	**Sam** finishes dressing *Mobile phone rings until* **Mal** *answers it*	(Page 4)
Cue 8	**Mal**: "Bunch of shirt lifters." *Mobile phone rings until* **Mal** *answers it*	(Page 9)
Cue 9	**Jill** points remote control at TV *TV voice sounds*	(Page 14)
Cue 10	**Jill** immediately mutes the sound on the TV *TV voice stops*	(Page 15)
Cue 11	**Jill** exits *Background drone of showroom muzak*	(Page 15)
Cue 12	**Dean** exits *Muzak fades out*	(Page 16)

Cue 13   **Jill** and **Chrissie** exit   (Page 17)
         Muzak plays

Cue 14   **Dean** hurries off after **Mal**   (Page 18)
         Muzak fades out

Cue 15   **Chrissie**: "Mum?"   (Page 19)
         Muzak plays

Cue 16   **Mal**: "I have to go out, after all …"   (Page 20)
         Muzak fades out

Cue 17   **Chrissie** exits   (Page 22)
         Muzak plays

Cue 18   **Dean** exits   (Page 23)
         Muzak fades out

Cue 19   **Mal**: "Enough to break your heart, isn't it?"   (Page 32)
         Car horn sounds outside

Cue 20   **Mal** points remote control at the TV   (Page 34)
         Loud burst of cheesy TV music

Cue 21   **Mal** points remote control at the TV again   (Page 34)
         TV music stops

Cue 22   **Jill** continues with her face   (Page 34)
         *Lavatory seat slams up, sounds of Mal relieving himself,
            brushing teeth, etc.*

Cue 23   **Jill** and **Mal** lie in bed for a while   (Page 35)
         Alarm sounds

Cue 24   **Mal** cancels the alarm   (Page 35)
         Alarm stops

ACT II

Cue 25   **Jill** starts to fill the kettle   (Page 40)
         Mal *relieves himself*

Cue 26   **Sam** serves himself some cornflakes   (Page 41)
         Mobile phone rings

Cue 27   **Mal:** "Dear, oh dear. Men!"   (Page 48)
         Mobile phone rings